The
SABIAN
MANUAL
MARC EDMUND JONES

MARC EDMUND JONES

SABIAN PUBLISHING SOCIETY
in association with
SHAMBHALA PUBLICATIONS

The SABIAN MANUAL

A Ritual for Living

STANWOOD, 1976

BOULDER

SABIAN PUBLISHING SOCIETY
2324 Norman Road
Stanwood, Washington 98292
in association with
SHAMBHALA PUBLICATIONS INC.
1123 Spruce Street
Boulder, Colorado 80302

BOOKS BY MARC EDMUND JONES — HOW TO LEARN ASTROLOGY • THE GUIDE TO HOROSCOPE INTERPRETATION • HORARY ASTROLOGY • ASTROLOGY, HOW AND WHY IT WORKS • THE SABIAN SYMBOLS IN ASTROLOGY • ESSENTIALS OF ASTROLOGICAL ANALYSIS • SCOPE OF ASTROLOGICAL PREDICTION • MUNDANE PERSPECTIVES IN ASTROLOGY • HOW TO LIVE WITH THE STARS • THE SABIAN BOOK • OCCULT PHILOSOPHY • GEORGE SYLVESTER MORRIS • *IN PREPARATION:* FUNDAMENTALS OF NUMBER SIGNIFICANCE.

Distributed in the United States by Random House and in Canada by Random House of Canada Ltd.

Printed in the United States of America

CONTENTS

THE RITUALS

APPENDIX

The advance is outward

The leadership is inward

The victory is to the broadest vision

THE SABIAN IDEA

This book has been prepared as a manual for the self-discipline provided by the age-old tradition of a Solar Mysteries, and also as a guide for anyone wishing to investigate the project of which this discipline is a part. Whether the individual encountering the Sabian presentation for the first time is one who seeks the discipline, or is merely the investigator, he is likely to find the materials and procedures somewhat baffling. This usually is so because of the large number of terms with which he will be unfamiliar, and because the methods of analysis or forms of judgment are alien to his experience.

The broad use of unfamiliar words may well be the first and major problem in any approach to this threshold of the Solar Mysteries. Indeed, many a person seeking a greater self-realization has been frightened away before he has given himself half a chance to know the fascinating vistas of mind and heart just within the portal. Actually a rather considerable vocabulary of exact terms can be mastered simply enough if the Sabian materials are handled in the light of the explanations given at length in the course of these pages. Nothing unusual is involved. A special terminology, and an accompanying precision of usage, are to be found in any area of modern specialization. The sciences have a huge array of technical terms. This is the case to hardly lesser extent in the arts, in manufacture and business, and wherever there must be communication with a minimal possibility of error in connection with any complex structure or function. Every individual entering a new line of work will expect to learn hundreds of extra words in order to refer intelligently to things with which he must deal, and if he is a specialist the hundreds may be thousands.

A second and related problem in an initial approach to the Sabian materials is not so much a matter of the terms themselves as the characteristic and perhaps altogether unfamiliar way in which they are used, and also at times the method of employing even the short and simple words of everyday life. No matter which of man's myriad languages may be made the basis of a true occult writing, in order that anything of the sort may be able to convey the eternal insights or report the actualities of a deeper spiritual experience, there is an inescapable necessity for presenting the pertinent ideas in the interweaving pattern of relationship that permits the mind to keep them framed in its own transcendental orientation. This mode of communication is the cabala, and an understanding of its operation has never been beyond the powers of a person of average ability. Aspirants without a high-school education have entered the Sabian discipline, and through a grasp of simple cabalistic principles have brought great richness to their lives. Moreover they have accomplished this without any excessive agony of soul or strain on their capacity for understanding. While a broad intellectual training can be a very great help in approaching the Solar Mysteries, it also can prove an insurmountable obstacle if it endows its possessor with any blind pride of knowledge.

Where the exactions of the cabala on first encounter in English seem anything but justified is in the complicated sentence structure. If the language were more highly inflected the difficulty would disappear. However, the price of the simpler sentences in that one respect would be the loss of an extraordinary fluidity of insight, such as is sustained in both oral and written communication by the position of terms in their sequence with each other. The formulas of expression that constitute the heart of cabalistic English have created an exceptional means for the enlightenment of the human mind, and have made it possible to achieve in years what often has required the labors of a lifetime. And here, of course, is the area of understanding in which the student may come to realize why an Ibn Gabirol had to formulate his conceptions in Arabic rather than the cognate Hebrew, or a Paul make his contribution in Greek rather than the Semite tongues of his day or a Blavatsky in English rather than French, German or Russian, and so on.

A third problem at the Sabian threshold of the Solar Mysteries is one to which a newcomer is not likely to be sensitive in his initial experience with the materials. But when he continues his investigation, and gains a measure of familiarity with the special vocabulary and the cabalistic sentence, he may find he has encountered a subtle and wholly subjective sort of resistance to his progress. It is here, even more than at actual first approach, that he may be frightened away from the Solar path. What he has started to realize now is the uncompromising flux of the ideas presented to him, together with the accompanying and practical fact that things progressively decline to stay put in any familiar fashion. In time he will understand that without special effort at extrication on his part, and probably without considerable help and encouragement from others of both the present and the past, he is forever caught in the hopeless circling of his acts and reactions. This repetitiveness of experience, known to occultists as karma, has given him an illusion of stability. He has been conditioned in a way of going that in natural course has become his bondage.

In order that he may be extricated from the impasse, or that his limitations or frustrations may be transformed into a more gratifying sustainment and release of the self's true powers in a karma of his own choosing, he must be helped to an alignment with a more productive frame of reality. This is possible when the basic indeterminacy of the real can be demonstrated to him. At the beginning the consideration of abstractions in this fashion is likely to seem little more than a senseless playing with words. Is it necessary to speak of indeterminacy? And what is meant by the real? However, it should at least be possible for him to realize that his mind may be helped to its own rebirth, and to expect that mental birth pangs may be as painful as physical. And it can be pointed out that the procedure is far from difficult in overview, although any practical achievement of the goal may require much more than the ideal minimum ten years of effort.

As preamble let it be said that the ultimate point of reference in any instruction, discussion or reflection is the individual seeker. In consequence it must be remembered at all times that whatever is written or spoken occultly or with universal reference must mean all things to all people, and hence different things to different people as well as different things to the same person at different times. The phenomenon is evident when several hundred Christian denominations in the United States base their common and opposing beliefs on the one occultly written Bible. What is vital in this is not the spread of implication, but rather the immutable pertinency of it to the mind in each particular aspect of spiritual orientation. To reapply the principle enunciated by Jesus in respect to the Sabbath, the fundamental question here is whether man properly is the possessor or the victim of the meanings in his experience. Thus the mastery of meaning is made of first importance in Sabian procedures.

The Sabian policy is not to make its presentations simple, if that requires that they be left no better than sterile, but rather is to persuade the seeker to approach the materials within the framework of his own understanding. Newcomers at the portal have always been told that while they might feel it would be helpful to have introductory lessons, these would defeat every real entrance into the Solar Mysteries. The methods have to be freed from regimenting helpfulness if they are to offer any release from life's hampering regimentations. In consequence there can be no (1) prescribed course through which everyone must pass, (2) fixed sequence of facts on which spiritual knowledge is to be built, or (3) uniform exercises that must be performed for the achievement of an immortal awakening. The situation of the Solar aspirant, in his occult rebirth, is like that of the baby born into physical existence. Any external reality has importance for him only in the experience of its entrance into his sharp-

ened consciousness. He must remember that whatever
stirs deep within himself is to have the initiative always,
and that at the start his concern with Sabian materials
should be entirely in accord with his mood of the moment.
He is not trying to go back to school any more than he
is attempting to re-enter his mother's womb. Rather he
is seeking to press forward into eternal understanding.
He is preparing himself for service in fellowship with the
Great Ones, and in consequence he should not try to stuff
himself with spiritual truth as though it were so much
pottage.

The Core of the Vocabulary

In general the Sabian presentation, in its use of the
exceptionally large number of terms needed to convey the
varying and fine shades of implication in its analyses, holds
as closely as possible to the meanings familiar in everyday life. With but the rarest exception a full dictionary
authority will be found for even the most technical distinctions. The rare coinage of a word, expansion of meaning or borrowing from some other language is always ac-
companied by repeated definition. There is, however, a
certain core of the Sabian vocabulary that can be summarized with advantage for anyone approaching the materials for a first time. It merely must be remembered that
points here treated very briefly or casually will have later
and detailed amplification. The terms to be noted are introduced in SMALL CAPITALS in the following paragraphs.

The whole body of principles, assumptions and facts
on which Sabian activities are based is designated as the
OCCULT TRADITION. ESOTERIC and ARCANE are used interchangeably with occult. EXOTERIC, SECULAR and ACADEMIC

are used for nonoccult. The Sabian project is identified formally as the SABIAN ASSEMBLY. As a school of thought it is the PHILOSOPHY OF CONCEPTS. As an initiatory organism it is said to be the SABIAN PORTAL OF THE SOLAR MYSTERIES. Reference to it commonly is as the SABIAN WORK or GROUP. Its administrative head is the CHANCELLOR, and an ESOTERIC SECRETARY takes care of routine details of the inner discipline. INNER as in distinction from OUTER identifies procedures or experiences of a subjective nature, or concerned with special obligations assumed for the purposes of initiation. SPIRITUAL, HIGHER and DEEPER are used with the same implication as inner. INITIATION is the expansion of consciousness that has for its end result the acquisition of the special knowledge and the development of the higher powers to which the occult tradition has always devoted itself in principal part. ILLUMINATION is an alternative term for initiation.

As capitalized SOLAR and LUNAR refer to the discipline of self at the hands of an authority recognized respectively as subjective or exercised from within the self and as objective or represented outwardly by a hierarchical establishment of ecclesiastical or similar sort. MYSTERIES is employed both for the advanced or more specialized knowledge of occultism and for the procedures in the investigation and acquisition of such a knowledge. ETERNAL WISDOM, or the ANCIENT WISDOM or the SECRET DOCTRINE interchangeably, refers according to context either to the ultimate potentiality of knowing as a species of racial intelligence or to the illimitability of knowing a man may activate for himself. OCCULT KNOWLEDGE identifies material of mind for which conventional verification is impossible.

The CANDIDATE for initiation is known interchangeably as the ASPIRANT, the SEEKER or the STUDENT. In special relationship to a personal teacher or GURU he is a CHELA. Men who have achieved conscious immortality and remained active in spiritual work through an INVISIBLE FELLOWSHIP with those who will share it are identified as INITIATES or collectively as the IMMORTAL COMPANY or the GREAT ONES. The MASTERS or BROTHERS are initiates of this sort associated in the SOLAR LODGE, and this group or its function is also identified as the GREAT WHITE LODGE or more simply as the LODGE. The SOLAR HIERARCH, or more simply the HIERARCH, is the Master or Brother with direct supervision over a channel of initiation such as the Sabian Assembly. His superior is the SOLAR ARCHON, or more simply the ARCHON and often alternatively the MAHACHOHAN. An ADEPT is an initiate in the exercise of thaumaturgic powers. An AVATAR is a world saviour and of high initiatory rank. The stages of growth or progress under Sabian auspices on the PATH OF INITIATION, often abbreviated as the PATH, are in order the NEOPHYTE, or the candidate first pledging himself to work for occult illumination, the ACOLYTE, or candidate undertaking special psychological drills after his initial orientation to the occult concepts, and the LEGATE, or candidate thereafter accepting particular meditative and ritualistic responsibilities. In the Sabian work a stage of LAY BROTHER is recognized as beyond legate status, but candidates of more than legate achievement are identified to those of lesser development than themselves as legates.

LAYA CENTER conveniently identifies the persisting reality of an original potential. It is the potentiality in question as it is able, without any compromising of its initially unlimited and unconditioned possibilities, to channel any pertinent and dynamic stimulus to the execution of itself. It is the nothing that constitutes the continuum or the core genius of every particular something, and in its active rather than passive role in experience it is the archetype of entity per se. It is order as an organism rather than a mechanism or a metaphysical reality. It is place without extension in space when such concomitantly is moment without extension in time, i.e., it is point as impingement of anything identified by time and space as within a time-and-space context. Thus virtually beyond definition, and gaining its great usefulness from that fact, the term is one of the very few from Sanskrit used by occultism but not to be found in the English dictionary. The basic idea is expressed also in THOUGHT FORM, although with too much implication of substance to be of equivalent value, and in the PHILOSOPHER'S STONE as the psychological actuality.

WORK IN CONSCIOUSNESS is effort centered in or at a laya center, and it is the entire foundation of Sabian healing on the one hand and of Solar initiation on the other. It has a more common designation as MEDITATION, or alternatively as CONCENTRATION, RETROSPECTION and COMMUNION. SOURCE and CENTER refer to the laya center of selfhood in its ultimate totality, and Source as capitalized also refers to deity. CHAKRAS are areas in the physical body that facilitate the powers of laya center in varying specific reference.

A RECENSION in characteristic Sabian usage is a paraphrase of sacred writings prepared to facilitate the re-

hearsal of spiritual experience. A SIGNATURE is the object
or event that stimulates the mind to the recognition of
heightened potentials in experience. MAGIC SQUARES are
suggestive arrangements of concepts on the pattern of the
mathematician's squares from which the term is taken,
and they borrow no less of course from the somewhat
similar word squares. QUADRANGLES are groups of four
students engaged in common work in consciousness.
KARMA and DHARMA are terms much used in Theosophy
for the prevailing or over-all patterns of obligation and
opportunity respectively in the life of the aspirant. ROOT
RACES and SUBRACES are designations of the human LIFE
STREAM in evolution on the globe in the dimensions of
tens of thousands and mere thousands of years respectively,
on the scale provided by the present focus of history.
WORLDS and PLANES are an over-all designation of areas of
dimension in time-and-space existence and experience respectively. ACTIVITY, SUBSTANCE and FORM are basic dis-
tributive terms for all-manifestation in its possible aspects.
TAROT is a technique of occult divination and analysis
through playing cards. The CABALA has been introduced,
but its wide variety of spellings should be noted as in
kabbalah or qabbala. The term MYOB is coined from the
first letters in the injunction, mind your own business.

The author's *Occult Philosophy* (New York, Sabian
Publishing Society, 1947) includes a glossary of more than
a thousand of the terms found most frequently in the
occult literature.

The Word Sabian

The use of the word Sabian to designate the present
project was a gradual development. The author employed

the term originally in his *Key Truths of Occult Philosophy* (Los Angeles, J. F. Rowny, 1925), to identify the fifth Atlantean subrace. By the time he came to rewrite and expand the earlier text as *Occult Philosophy*, a recognition of the Sumerians as typical of the racial substream seemed to promise a more helpful orientation in what still remains an almost insuperable problem of charting. In the meanwhile the first attempt at an improved patterning for the races had given the word its special association with the occult brotherhood under whose auspices the group was taking form. Its adoption as a name for the work, then fairly well in progress, was a curiously casual contribution of the students in the California classes.

There has long been a marked confusion between Sabaean and Sabian. The former identifies the star-worshipers of the ancient Near East, and may arise from Saba or Sheba. This was the kingdom made familiar to history by its queen, who visited Solomon in order to investigate the quality of his wisdom. There is a likely relationship between Sabaean and Sabaoth, or the hosts in the designation of God as Lord of Hosts. These hosts would be armies literally, but in more important and symbolical reference they were the stellar myriads that represented the powers of heaven. Sabian, which would translate roughly as Baptist, probably refers to the Gnostic Mandaeans or Observants of St. John the Baptist more commonly and improperly known as the Christians of St. John. Its significance stems from the fact that these Sabians were included with the Jews and Christians in the Koran as the three groups entitled to tolerance. In selecting his earlier term for the Atlantean subrace the author had Sabaean in mind.

As it happened, the authority on which he relied at the time preferred the spelling Sabian for which there is indeed some recognition, and this accident of less than the best scholarship proved a fortuitous circumstance.

The city of Harran in Mesopotamia was a frontier place of importance long before Abraham's people stopped there and so of course before his son and grandson made the journey back to select wives of the idealized close relationship. As a seat for the worship of the moon god Sin it created an effective foundation for the Lunar Mysteries of what then was perhaps the fifteenth century, B.C., and it became a famous center of magic from the time of Alexander the Great until the coming of the Mongols in the thirteenth century A.D. In the ninth century it faced real trouble when the Caliph Mamun threatened to destroy it unless its people either embraced Islam or convinced him their beliefs and practices were entitled to toleration. On the advice of a Mohammedan jurist they identified themselves as Sabian. Nobody knew what the designation implied, despite the Koran's favorable attitude, and in consequence the Harranites were able to continue in their usual ways. Under the necessity to have a holy book, they adopted the writings of Hermes or the traditional collections of Egyptian lore, and ultimately this arbitrary ordering of their speculations must have been quite instrumental in giving European occultism its characteristic slant in the later medieval period. The city became famous as a clearinghouse for the great final flame of the Arabian enlightenment, and thus its inhabitants blessed the name they adopted and in their achievements they truly challenge the present Sabian group.

THE SABIAN ASPIRANT

The Sabian project in its origins was a purely individual questing, and quite a side issue in comparison with the pursuit of wholly conventional religious interests. Indeed, there was little to suggest that what seemed a casual curiosity might in time give rise to group effort and perhaps develop an over-all potential of real significance.

The first identifiable beginning of any objective nature was the author's letter to the *Chicago Evening Post*, on February 6, 1912, requesting information on astrology. In the reply he was told that he was superstitious, and should beware of fortunetellers, but he had taken an initial step in his investigation of the occult. He was about to become the pioneer Sabian aspirant of this present age, and for a full decade he would remain the only one. His move to Los Angeles in November, 1913, and his acquaintance with Ella Woods in connection with his motion-picture writing, brought him in touch with a competent astrologer. Her interpretation of his horoscope led to the astrological researches that have occupied a large share of his time ever since. On October 17, 1914, his experience in what occultists usually describe as a meeting with a Master in the flesh led to his working contacts with Theosophy and then in train with New Thought, Spiritualism and an ever-widening world of transcendental literature and activities.

His inquiries in these occult areas remained entirely personal, however, until a rather persistent demand from a number of friends for practical information on astrological theory and methods resulted in an informal gathering and the start in a transition to group effort. The meetings were in New York City and they continued every other week from December 5, 1922, until April of the following year. During these sessions the author became aware of an effective and living contact with intelligences of long prior generations and proceeded to enlist them in what gradually became identified as the Sabian project. The investigation of the Eternal Wisdom under these occult auspices led back to what at the time were identified as Babylonian sources but which subsequently have been found to be more characteristically Sumerian. The developing scope of this new mode of research, which originally was largely of a spiritualistic nature, was dramatic demonstration of the value of collective as against merely individual effort. With the co-operation of many minds and the mobilization of a vast range of skills in the group, the chances of unsuspected error were reduced very considerably. Indeed, it had become all too obvious that the work had taken on a complexity requiring more than the author's unaided efforts. On October 17, 1923, in Los Angeles, what is now the Sabian Assembly had its tangible beginning in a class that he conducted under the sponsorship of Manly Palmer Hall at the Church of the People.

The original emphasis in the classwork was astrological, both in New York in 1922 and in California the following year, but before long the scope of attention broadened to embrace virtually every phase of occultism. Thus in the

latter part of 1924 there was a study of the arcane principles built into the Biblical book of Daniel, and brought
to a fascinating simplicity as incorporated in the structure
of Grimms' fairy tales. 1925 saw the publication of the
author's *Key Truths of Occult Philosophy*, or the master
thesis under the Solar Mysteries that qualified him as a
genuine occultist for this incarnation. In October, 1926,
came the first tentative translation and exposition of the
all-important *Fons Vitae* of Solomon ben Judah ibn
Gabirol, and this led in time to the complete commentaries on Plato, Aristotle and Plotinus. During the first
Los Angeles years there was an intimate and warm association with Walter Raymond, Frederic W. Keeler and
William Walker Atkinson, leading to an intensified interest and activity in the New Thought field. The more
formal Bible studies began in 1926 and perhaps the final
stage of basic orientations was reached with the formation
in San Diego, shortly after the Sabian symbols for the zodiacal degrees were created, of the Spiritualistic church of
which Elsie Wheeler was pastor and the author president.

The association with Theosophy has been part and
parcel of the author's inner life from earliest childhood.
Because of the depth of the relationship it did not take
form until in the 1930's, when a series of summer conferences of exceptional inspiration was held at Halcyon,
California, in co-operation with the Temple of the
People. Ties with Jennie E. Bollenbacher in the following decade resulted finally in his literal and continuing
affiliation with the Columbus, Ohio, Lodge of the Adyar
Theosophical Society. The more personal details of his
struggle of mind and heart toward the insights on which

the Sabian project could be founded, and as seen in the orthodox rather than heterodox context of his life, are summarized in the foreword of his *George Sylvester Morris* (New York, Sabian Publishing Society, 1948).

The Sabian Assembly

As the Sabian Assembly has come into being and established its various procedures it has sought to avoid all overemphasis of particular directions of interest. Thus astrology, as one of the most exacting of the areas of study and investigation, is kept an option for student attention. In practice the stellar analysis never seems to become the concern of more than half the active membership, although it remains of fundamental import in the project. All possible phases of human experience are known to have their full part in the significance of the whole, however, no matter how potential this may have to be in the given instance.

At the beginning the author had envisioned a thoroughly informal gathering of people who would have a background in occult knowledge and experience and who could be found wherever his literary work might take him. In a way this was an adaptation of the seminar idea, and there are still those who look on the Sabian activities as a sort of graduate school of the transcendental realizations. It soon became evident, however, that the procedures and goals could hardly be educational in any established pattern if there was to be any possibility of breaking through either the unsuspected presuppositions of mind or the little-realized limitations of heart so characteristic of the age. A true occult inquiry to have enduring worth would have to cut across all lines of intellectual or cultural distinctions. Therefore it was necessary to learn what could have equal appeal to every mind from the most stunted to the most brilliant, and what could bring self-fulfillment of equivalent value both to the person little able to exert himself for his own well-being and to the one surcharged with ambition for position or creative effectiveness. In consequence no single type of individual could be seen as being more fit for Sabian participation than any other. New ground would have to be broken to achieve any real breadth of constituency, and the basis for this breadth would have to be an uncompromising respect for human personality.

The orientation to formal religion has been a problem from the first change-over from an individual to a group development of the project. It was realized from the outset that the Assembly above all else must avoid becoming a cult, and so demanding adherence to some special body of beliefs. To operate in competition with any identifiable form of faith would be to exclude every real contribution of transcendent realization, other than those of the type thereupon accepted by the Sabian aspirants for their unification in the particular direction of outreach. The orthodoxy thus set up would defeat the spiritual end in view before a single effective step could be taken toward its achievement. But because of this necessity a question arises very promptly. How can religious things be studied profitably without a genuine experience with them?

One procedure encouraged very commonly in occultism is the participation in religious allegiances and ceremonies with the assumption of a personal possession of deeper and more inward insights, and a consequent winnowing of what is true or false according to the self-endowed and private superiority. Such infiltration is not only no actual acceptance of the beliefs and practices to which attention is given but in its essential dishonesty is a complete stultification of every spiritual aspiration. The seeker on the path must approach the doctrines and usages of any and every church with the same respect he is expected to show for personality in its individual manifestation through each of his fellows. This means that he must recognize an illumination and a complete sufficiency of revealed source in every form of religion he may approach as a basis for worship, and must remember that he can gain an experience of its reality only as he is able to give testimony to its eternal potentialties. He is not a zealot worming his way into a social institution in order to change or destroy it, or to make it a vehicle for something other than it is, but rather he is the preserver seeking the fulfillment of everything he touches through offering a contribution of at least some small measure of admiration for the genius of its being.

Quite as great as the basic difficulties of the underlying intellectual and religious orientations of the group members, in the transition from a purely personal advancement of the project to the co-operative working out of its potentials, has been the perfecting of the necessary mechanics of organization in a way that will not contribute to an ultimate ineffectiveness and dissolution. All human history seems to demonstrate that when authority is formalized, and established at some central point, the result is an increasing diversion of every energy and resource from the major goal to the perpetuation and increase of the power and its prerogatives at the center of administration. Such a core of crystallization is fatal to all actual progress or growth. The author as an individual had no difficulty keeping the operation of the project as fluid as he wished, and the earlier achievements that in embryo have proved to be an exceptionally correct anticipation of everything later brought to more detailed focus in understanding and applicability are unquestionably due to the basic fluidity of the effort. Nothing is accomplished in a vacuum, but little more is achieved in a senseless complex of limitations.

Above all else it has been necessary to bring to the Assembly a freedom from needless groovings of mind and unthinking acceptances of prejudice, since this freedom alone can be a basis for any wide and unlimited participation in both speculative and actual experience. The vision has been of an organic or momentarily convenient rather than of a mechanical or rigid ordering of thought and impression. To dramatize the policy the project has been identified almost from the start as a philosophical laboratory, or something that of itself is largely nothing in order that it may serve the ends in view more impartially. In the years of functioning continuity, from the inception of the group down to the moment of present writing, the details of operation have been given definite organization only to the extent of unquestioned necessity. A general headquarters has been avoided. Tasks such as the editorial work on materials and their preparation and distribution, arrangements for meetings or conferences, and indeed every possible operation of the project, have been left in the hands of the volunteer workers among the students.

For the volunteers in Sabian service there is no worldly
remuneration. The Chancellor and others in whom tangible or commonplace authority is vested are not expected
to derive any payment for their effort from Sabian funds
or from any form of assessment of their fellows. Free interchange of a genuine fellowship is seen to be hampered
by conventional incentives or rewards. True spiritual
effort cannot found or operate a business. Occult participation in the reality of man's day-by-day manipulation
of physical needs and goods must be on transcendental
levels.   Thus matters of the essential or practical categories such as the cost of lessons, traveling and the publication of books and the like are handled in a fashion
proper to the time and conditions, but always with the
irreducible minimum of mechanical organization.

In the light of all this it might well be expected that
the details of group establishment and method should be a
result of gradual growth, and that each procedure should
unfold or be created as need arises. The Full Moon ceremony, adapted from the Church of the New Civilization
of the author's friend and true voice of the Eternal Wisdom, Julia Seton, was given Sabian form spontaneously
as conducted for a first time in the Hollywood Studio of
Philosophy. The system of pledges was inaugurated in
1926 when the expulsion of two members of the Los
Angeles class from the inner section of a Rosicrucian
group, for their refusal to drop the classwork, in a sense
challenged the Assembly-in-evolution to provide a full-
scale initiation for any seekers anywhere who otherwise
might be denied it. It was at this time that a charter was
obtained from the Great White Lodge, to explain the

event in the manner usually adopted by occultists, and the group's lily-and-snake symbol was then delivered as the hallmark of the special authority. The healing ministry came into being in a simple clarification of the New Thought patterns, and all later details of procedure have developed in the step-by-step outreaching toward the vision of a collective destiny.

Membership in the Assembly

The real life and being of the Sabian Assembly are in the necessarily intangible participation of its members collectively in what occultism knows as an invisible fellowship. This is a term that has come into currency to emphasize the continual relationship maintained by the aspirant with the Great Ones who in their transcendental living have created man's spiritual history. The degree to which the individual student may be aware of this relationship, and be able in consequence to profit from it consciously, will vary of course in each case and in accordance with the particular stage of growth in understanding or of psychological unfoldment.

By participation in the invisible fellowship is meant more specifically the expenditure of effort and the development of aspiration directed in common toward the achievement of the goals envisioned in the spiritual history of the race, both for each person in his own right and collectively for all. It is said to be invisible because it reaches from mind to mind and from heart to heart without intervention or mediation by any tangible or limiting agency of any sort, and it is a fellowship because there is no possibility of quickening any such higher potential of human experience without a free sharing of whatever may come

through its gaining. By spiritual is meant no more than
illimitable, or that which is above and beyond the time-
and-space lattice of involvement. The seeker comes to
realize that it is through the involvements of so-called
lower reality that men come to know their needless separations and blind competitions, and so find themselves
arrayed against each other in lack of understanding and
enmity.

Membership in the Assembly is contingent on a positive
desire to participate in the invisible fellowship, and to
have a role of at least some significance in furthering its
goals. As a first step the aspirant must sign the Sabian
neophyte pledge and assume a proper share of responsibility for the physical costs of the project. As a second and
continuing step he must give faithful attention to the
lesson materials, and in addition and before too long he
should accept some one or more of the opportunities offered for specialized services and ramifying forms of self-
dedication or increasing contribution of energy and
means.

Since the invisible fellowship in its immediate reality is
cradled in the practical world of everyday, where the prevailing cultural patterns add the psychological necessities
of personal existence to the more obvious physiological
ones, all Sabian procedures are shaped to further a personal well-being in simple and effective fashion as an initial and vital foundation for the higher aspiration. The
foundational necessities are seen as (1) ordinary health,
(2) economic freedom and (3) emotional aplomb. Obviously they are the three main elements of human fulfillment in its lowest terms, and to them is added under-

standing as the privilege of a self-satisfaction on a some-what higher level. These four consummations are the re-wards the aspirant has the right to expect from the begin-ning as a result of his aspiration. They are the answers to the world, and its questions of the why of spiritual seeking, when perspectives are limited to a time-and-space context.

The true aspirant, however, must know that he is en-tering a fellowship with those like-minded in reaching out to broader spiritual ends in which the destiny of a race and a globe may be said to rest. He must realize that he is expected to do his part in sustaining the rhythms of a transcendental group consciousness in all its interweaving manifestations. Here is something he may not come to understand in full until after considerable development of his insights, and indeed as a consequence of endless and often puzzling experience with the unrealized intricacies of both human nature and the cosmic constitution. None-theless he may gain a valuable and simple orientation at the start, and realize its validity through the subtle if not exactly comprehensible self-strengthening he can identify within himself at core. The heart of the Solar Mysteries since time immemorial has been an uncompromising loyalty to its ritual, and there is direct parallel here to the implication of the prophet Ezekiel that faithlessness in the rehearsal of spiritual experience and of all self-committal is far more destructive to the ultimate welfare of the race than the crimes of everyday life for which society has sharp though transient punishment. In the outer cradling of its procedures in a normal experience of a present-day generation the Sabian Assembly therefore sets up its first

measure of an aspirant's performance in the regularity of
(1) his sharing of his means on the physical or foundational level and (2) his participation in Sabian thought
by his regular attendance at group discussion or his equally
regular reports by mail on his adventures with the lesson
materials.

Resignation from the Assembly is the right of the student at any time, since his original affiliation must be an
ever-continuing affirmative to be effective.. The surrender
of anything he has gained is its delivery back to the eternal
pool of human potentiality, and therefore no loss in any
possible sense, and his holding to what has seemed profitable in the refinement of his experience as an individual
should be both a compensation in full and a precise measure of what he has shared of himself. His actual contribution to the group continues in the reality of the whole
into which it has been built, and this is his spiritual reward whether he is aware of it or not. There are always
those who come into the fellowship briefly, and since they
leave on this equitable basis the chapter should end on
the same note of good will with which it began. However, resignation by mere cessation of the self-contribution
at full flood is the unforgivable sin of Biblical imagery,
and it may be fraught with extraordinary danger to the
seeker's immortal on-going.

Sometimes there will be those who through the discipline develop tangible skills and acquire knowledge that
they are able to employ better in channels other than
Sabian for the ultimate fulfillment of their own lives, as
well as for the discharge of their occult obligations. Their
endowment may prove of much greater value in projects

of a different esoteric slanting, or of more conventional philosophical, psychological or religious sort. Their completion of the initiatory self-development in the ideal ten years, or in whatever longer period may be required, need never constitute a commitment to continue as participant in the particular vision that has served them. At the core of the Sabian project, however, are the aspirants who through their training within the fellowship have come to deliver the whole of themselves and their potentials to its ends in view. Those in the work more transiently are quite as welcome, but the ultimate custodians of the greater dream are collectively what the Assembly can be said to be in its over-all terms. This inner company embraces the seeker of immortal dedication no less after than before his decease.

By the token of all this a member once resigning may come back to participation in the Assembly, and without prejudice. His turn to other orientations is merely a detail of his experience on the path, and he will not be penalized if he repeats the procedure or even does so many times over. Similarly there are those who like to traverse many ways to the Eternal Wisdom all at once, like the rider of two horses or driver of three or four in the ancient circus. To spread himself so thin is rather pointless for the average seeker, if not indeed a contribution to the total defeat of his objectives, but a true respect for personality requires that no objection be raised to the multiple affiliations. However, Sabian requirements must be met as conscientiously as in every other case.

The Sabian aspirant, after two years given to a faithful performance of the neophyte obligations, may enter the

acolyte discipline by signing the proper pledge form. The
substance of effort in this grade is the study of special lessons for the five acolyte years, and the performance of
special fortnightly drills of a psychological nature as these
are given in each of the special outlines. On arrival at
Lesson XXI in each of the five series there are two letters
to write as a condition of receiving the next series in order,
and of entering the legate work when acolyte-grade requirements have been met for the final time.

What is known as work in consciousness, consisting in
this case of meditation for at least five minutes daily on
matters in the interest of which the service is volunteered,
is a required detail of acolyte discipline. Neophytes meanwhile and at their option may participate in this labor of
the spirit as practice in preparation for acolyte enlistment.
For any dependable sustainment of the meditative ritual
the seeker must cradle his effort in the everyday reality of
which he is most fundamentally and genuinely a part.
This demands his understanding co-operation with the
prevailing mores as the sole basis on which a Solar Mysteries may operate. Hence there is a stress on a strict personal normality throughout the Sabian instruction. However, when a recasting or liberalization of current standards becomes the expression of his spiritual goal he must
live the life of active protest, as all reformers have had
to do of necessity in every age of man. But in general he
enhances his subjective contribution to the eternal vision
as he comports himself naturally and decently in the eyes
of his fellows, since in that fashion he best lifts their upward reach into a measure of assimilation to his own.
Each aspirant of course must make his own decisions as to

what his rules of conduct will involve. These may be in connection with the use of stimulants such as alcohol or tobacco, or tea and coffee, or even spices and condiments generally. Involved may be a resort to the time-tried methods of self-discipline such as fasting, breathing exercises, the refusal of food when life must be taken to provide it, sexual continence and a host of other practices that more frequently than not will have their normal setting in cultures other than his own. In every procedure of this nature the end in view of course is to endow experience with an increasing symbolization of eternal values.

Acolytes are asked to volunteer for three years of specific individual service to the Sabian Assembly, in addition to their general obligation, and this may be of tangible or intangible order as is acceptable in the given case to each of them and his particular mentor. In the course of the five years he selects a mystery name, and after its approval he may use it in all inner phases of group procedure. Its principal function is to remind him that in ultimate fact he is ever the conscious creator of his own true identity, and thus the actual arbiter of his destiny. Also and in due time he plants a fixed physical object as the symbolical nucleus of a laya center both for an invisible or immortal task and for his own initiate personality which in a sense will develop out of it. Thus he is provided in token fashion with a continual reminder that in his highest potentiality he is always linked necessarily, through wholly practical and common roots, with his fellows of even the least spiritual unfoldment.

The ritualistic core of acolyte discipline is attendance in person or by proxy at sixty-three consecutive Full

Moon meetings. There is no objection to the aspirant sending his proxy to some fellow-seeker in the discipline as a safeguard for the continuity and then also attending a ceremony in person. Similarly he may have proxies at more than one meeting. However, he is not permitted to make provision for more than one lunar month in advance, except in the case of protracted travel when communications may be unreliable. All performance of obligation by the neophyte is on honor and without check excepting only the regularity with which he shares his means, but the Full Moon attendance is made a matter of permanent record by the Chancellor or an esoteric secretary appointed by him to assist in administering the inner discipline.

Study groups for the acolytes are encouraged when there are students of this grade who can meet together in person, and it is permitted in any such gathering to change the order of the five sets of acolyte lessons for any one or more of those attending in order to increase the number of those coming together each two weeks. However, the requirements of Lesson XXI for the acolyte must always be as put down for the year of discipline to which he actually belongs, and by the same token he should perform the fortnightly drills proper to his stage of progress. Candidates for acolyte work may sign their pledges as much as six months in advance if their participation in the special classwork is facilitated as a result, but the required attendance at a Full Moon ceremony sixty-three consecutive times in special ritualistic self-realization cannot begin until the time of actual acolyte eligibility. If there is a break in meeting this requirement, so that it is not completed at the time of legate eligibility otherwise, that discipline may be undertaken and this detail of acolyte obligation met concurrently. If necessary or desirable an acolyte may take an additional year or more for any of the five sections of the work without penalty other than loss of time.

Acolyte study groups may be started at intervals and at times determined by the Chancellor, but the ritual for the quarterly meetings is adjusted to April and October as times of particular and symbolical efficacy for the cycles of acolyte discipline. It is not necessary that acolyte classes be led or taught by someone further advanced in occult training, but no member of the Sabian Assembly may serve an acolyte group as teacher or leader if he himself has not signed an acolyte pledge.

After his five acolyte years the student may enter the legate grade for the three or more years he may need for his continuing spiritual refinement. He takes the step by signing the legate pledge, after the completion of all necessary acolyte requirements excepting perhaps the attendance at Full Moon meetings. As the ritualistic token of this new dimension of effort he undertakes to spend an hour in special inner communion immediately before each of twelve consecutive quarterly meetings, and either to attend them or to have an excuse from the Chancellor or esoteric secretary in advance. For him an Easter eve gathering takes the place of the public quarterly meeting on Palm Sunday. The restricted esoteric occasion on the Saturday evening becomes the annual focus for a course of development that by long tradition and of necessity remains oral in nature. With the mouth-to-ear communication the aspirant encounters the symbolical or ritualistic secrecy that is perhaps best known to the world at large through the procedures of Freemasonry. There is nothing in the work of a Masonic Lodge that is not to be found printed openly in books, although the master mason faithful to his pledges will never certify to the correctness or incorrectness of any details made public. His lips are sealed for the integrity of himself and his companions in the creation of an invisible fellowship that in potentiality at least is as encompassing as the occult Mysteries.

Sabian aspirants of legate grade are aggregated in quadrangles. Each quadrangle consists of four seekers who work together in consciousness for something of common concern, in the same manner they have been carrying meditative responsibility singly as acolytes. It is the privilege of acolytes to form in these groups of four as a practice in advance of legate procedures, and in such a case they may seek to further the larger-dimension goals they can envision through their common effort. A quadrangle remains in existence as long as all four participants continue in their desire to work together. At a regular time of assignment to the quadrangles, preferably annually, all qualified members of the Assembly are given an opportunity to enlist by means of written and confidential forms sent directly to the Chancellor or esoteric secretary. Any given quadrangle is dissolved unless the legates or acolytes comprising it elect to continue their work together. All new quadrangle assignments are worked out by interview or correspondence with the Chancellor or esoteric secretary. The successful formation of quadrangles, and the approvals of special work in consciousness for which aspirants volunteer singly, are reported to those concerned

in writing or by special form letters issued to the students
undertaking this service. Legates who wish may invite
acolytes to provisional place in their quadrangles. Surviving legates of quadrangles including fellow-workers of
legate grade who have deceased may continue the invisible
fellowship without exterior alteration by electing to do
so at each annual enlistment.

Under the Sabian presentation of the Solar Mysteries
the achievement of higher grades of initiation such as lay
brother is never admitted except orally and in the company of those of equal or greater experience in the ritualistic self-refinement, and the classification of legate is used
to embrace everything above acolyte. This practice is in
conformity with the realization that anything after all is
what it does, and that the doing in the instance of exalted
spiritual responsibilities is really more apparent in fruits
that can be recognized by all men and so realized in their
scope by the widespread evidence of their value. Distinctions among personalities on a transcendental level are
altogether meaningless because an individual when he becomes more and more All-Self in particular respects has
little of mere selfhood about which any intelligent statement can be made. The advance on the Solar path is not
into mystery and confusion. Rather it is into a greater
clarification marked ultimately by an understanding that
is universal because all men may possess it, and that is
eternal because no time can be more pregnant than the
present. Initiation in actuality is never more than the
expansion of consciousness that the smallest child can
know in simple fashion, but that the wisest adult may lose
in the higher potential simply because of his unnatural

fear of self-transcending experience. Therefore it is said in the Bible that the kingdom of heaven belongs to the children.

Secrecy under the Sabian presentation of the Solar Mysteries in consequence is ever a drill in the subjective expansion of an all-awareness rather than any hiding of things. Since what is to be expanded should be worth the effort by every possible standard, the individual is expected to come before the eternal portal with clean hands as in spiritual parallel to the requirement of appeal to a court in equity under United States law. The respect for personality on which the Assembly is built is expressed most frequently in the demand that each seeker mind his own business in a very literal sense. And by the same token he knows that his fellows are not to take over his unfoldment nor are to seek to help him except as he invites them to do so. The Assembly does not concern itself over the private lives of its members, and asks no questions as to other interests. The participant in the invisible fellowship is merely expected to do the proper thing, whether for himself or the work, and to do this without being told. He is taken as adult, since otherwise he is not ready for genuine initiation. If there are things he needs to know about the work, he should be mature enough to make the necessary inquiry or to gain the information he wishes by observation and a perusal of the materials. And if he does not contribute to the morale of the work by respecting the intelligence of its procedures and endeavoring to understand them through a resort to common sense if nothing else, he is destroying his own spiritual potential by the betrayal of the leading that brought him to the Sabian portal of the Eternal Wisdom.

If freedom and respect demanded for his own personality are twisted around by an aspirant, to become a threat to the freedom of his fellows and a lack of respect for their personalities, the organic integrity of the Assembly is at stake and therefore it has every right to take whatever action may be needed to protect itself. Thus conduct that offers any least outrage to the immediate community or to the prevailing culture can never be tolerated. The use of common activities for purposes of political propaganda or subversive behavior in any possible implication of the term is contrary to all Sabian purposes. Personal solicitation as a part of business or financial promotion in any form in association with Sabian activities is a perversion of their function. As the Assembly teaches in general so must it practice in particular. It must not only be sure that it minds its own business but that its members do likewise while taking part in its procedures.

In addition to the regular Sabian pledged students of the neophyte, acolyte and legate grades there are also non-pledged participants or individuals who desire to share in the studies and general activities but who do not care to undertake the spiritual or subjective side of the discipline. These members of the student body are entitled to receive all neophyte materials and to have all neophyte privileges, provided they meet Sabian standards of conduct and make a monthly contribution that covers at least the estimated cost of carrying a regular student on the roll.

At any time after two years in the work a pledged student of any grade may transfer to the alumni group and make his contribution on the basis of the lesser costs incurred in his case. He will receive no further lessons but will continue to get all other materials of regular issue. He will have the privileges of his grade and may take his part in all inner or spiritual activities, as in keeping his place on a legate or acolyte quadrangle. He may transfer back to active status without prejudice whenever he wishes to do so.

Students in the astrological discipline receive an extra weekly lesson on the stellar science, and they are asked to share of their means on the basis of the higher cost of carrying them on the roll. They are not distinguished from the nonastrological members of the Assembly in any other respect.

Junior aspirants are boys and girls who sign a special pledge with the approval of parents or guardians, at any time before their fifteenth birthday, and who undertake to perform some specific and tangible service in some phase of the Sabian project as a token of their interest. If faithful in the performance of this for at least two years they may, on their fifteenth birthday or thereafter, become regular members of the Assembly by signing the neophyte pledge. If they wish they also may enter the acolyte work by signing the acolyte pledge simultaneously. In general the junior obligation needs the stimulus of direct association with adult activities, as in connection with a study group or some objective Sabian enterprise.

Students afield are members in all categories of the Assembly who are unable to carry on their Sabian activities in company with others, or who do not care to do so. At the beginning they may have much greater difficulty in getting into the rhythm of the work, but in the long run they may develop a much greater creative strength within themselves. They lose the chance to participate in the rehearsal of spiritual experience through the discussion group, together with the greater immediateness of insight that follows when the two or three are gathered in the ineffable name for their devotions and a release of the self's potentials. Ultimately they gain their place in the invisible fellowship more directly in touch with the great souls who never can be reached as intimately through the ramification of focus when a number have met together, and in consequence there may be a more immediate flowering of the eternal self-reliance on which a conscious immortality depends. With less opportunity for quick validations the students afield have more wonderful exercise of an untrammeled potentiality. Such aspirants participate in Sabian functioning no less and no more than those aspirants who walk perhaps more conveniently with their fellow seekers, but their initiative has to serve them more assiduously and in that fact there is spiritual power. Thus the disadvantages and advantages remain oddly in balance, and this has been true since the earliest years of the project.

The marriage partner of a student shares that student's status in every respect. When man and wife are both aspirants they are treated as a single individual in respect to the issue of materials and financial contributions, unless they prefer to have duplicate sets of lessons and to make separate offerings to the work.

Regular students in financial difficulties, provided they have been members in good standing of the Assembly for six months or more, may make full discharge of their obligation by token contributions monthly in the form of a stamp or small coin during their period of limitation. They are required, however, to participate in the healing ritual regularly and to ask spiritual aid in the amelioration of their situation as long as it continues.

Summary

The Sabian Assembly has its roots in the purely individual research of its founding chancellor. Its actual beginning was in private classwork a decade later. The Assembly dates the continuity of its existence from October 17, 1923.

Its subject of first interest was astrology, but its overall concern soon broadened to include every area of knowledge or experience that might lead to the Eternal Wisdom. Attention was directed to the Bible, to the world's philosophers with detailed studies of Plato and then of Aristotle and Plotinus for further development of Platonic insights, to New Thought with an adoption and continual refinement of the healing techniques of mental science, to the cabala as redeveloped for modern life on the basis of Ibn Gabirol's contribution, to symbolism in its ageless roots, to Theosophy and Spiritualism for their special impact on recent times, and to the occult traditions of the East and West in their ever-ramifying significance. Neither astrology nor any other one part of the whole has been permitted to dominate the vision.

To escape the limitations of prevailing educational conceptions the project was shaped to cut across all lines of intellectual distinction, since thereby it might hope to develop an understanding such as would have equal clarity for every mind from the least endowed to the most gifted.

To provide an impartial appreciation of all possible religious insights the approach has encouraged every creative participation in the various forms of faith, but without affirming a necessary primacy for any one of them and without denying the right of any individual to set up such a primacy for his own particular experience of God.

To keep the project creatively fluid it has been developed as an organism with members who are accepted as adult and who therefore not only are presumed to know the right thing to do but are expected to do it of their own volition. Organization has been avoided as far as possible. Practical details are handled according to prevailing custom and as the need arises. All procedures are built on an uncompromising respect for personality, and on a demand that each aspirant mind his own business or seek the kingdom of heaven for himself before venturing to promote it too assiduously for his fellows.

All rituals and methods arose through extemporization at the times they first proved useful, and this spontaneity has become the very essence of the project.

The life of the Sabian vision is in the invisible fellowship of common effort toward common goals on the transcendental levels of the tradition it has built into its own being, and in the consequent communion with the great souls who created the real genius of occultism in the past. Membership in the Assembly begins with an expressed desire to participate in this fellowship.

The higher ends sought are seen as being cradled in the lesser goods in which the mass of humanity of the world can share. Therefore the token of continuing aspiration is taken to be the achievement of a bodily health, an economic stability, a psychological poise and a desire for effective understanding on the level of everyday validations. Faithfulness in maintaining the rhythms of the work in its down-to-earth orientations is found to be the most important qualification for the more exalted self-perfecting. The labor of the spirit in consciousness is the fundamental strength of the Sabian enterprise, and the five minutes of daily meditation required of the aspirant early in the work merely prepare him for his more serious spiritual responsibilities in the group.

Members of the Sabian Assembly are given almost complete liberty to express themselves in their respective ways as they learn how best to participate in the project. Thus they may enter or leave the work at will and change status whenever they please, providing only that they meet the basic and simple requirements. There are varieties of affiliation and emphasis, and of adjustment to the personal situation.

After two years as a neophyte the aspirant may become an acolyte, and in this stage he has the obligation of special study for five years, of more directed work in consciousness, of psychological drills to perform and of details of discipline for developing his more specific self-unfoldment. In similar fashion and as a next step he may undertake legate work with three years of specific obligations of a generally more subjective sort. After that period there can be an endlessly continuing self-fulfillment, contingent on an indomitable desire to serve the highest spiritual vision.

THE SABIAN ORIENTATION

The over-all orientation of the Sabian project is to be found in the occult tradition. Occultism by most simple definition embraces the arts and practices dealing with supernatural influences and agencies, together with the knowledge concerning them. In consequence the term includes all manner of speculative approach to the unknown. Also and less happily this can be what often is a purely superstitious attraction to the unexplained phenomena, or a compulsive desire for magical powers and foreknowledge. Esoteric, as an alternative designation, has been favored by many occultists since its adoption by Pythagoras to identify that which enters in behind the sign or the outer manifestation of anything in question. Arcane comes from the arcanum of the alchemists, and has the same general meaning.

The Sabian project interprets the occult tradition as a special mode of understanding, or a way of particular self-dedication, that at least by its own account has had an unbroken continuity from the dawn of recorded history. The occultists, in the frame of the varying and unfolding cultures through which they have struggled toward a larger understanding of their world and themselves, have created a body of arcane insights which in recent centuries they have sought to share with all. Unfortunately their efforts in this direction have tended to defeat themselves through an insistence on the caste system for spiritual reality, while at the same time decrying it in political realms. As a result today's aspirant must realize that the lingering notions of a favoritism whereby some are deemed more worthy for receiving broader knowledge or greater powers than others, simply because of their circle of association or of their conformity to particular standards and acceptance of special beliefs, is a case of transforming a very simple fact of psychology into the needless complexity of moral issue. All fancy theories to the contrary, whatever man may have for his use or his enjoyment is never more than the fruits of the experience necessary to bring this into his possession.

The occult need not be regarded as differing in any appreciable respect from any other area of human interest and effort, unless perhaps in the depths and catholicity of its roots and of course and most importantly in the living continuance of its invisible fellowship. Actually it is impossible to draw very sharp lines of definition between the arcane realizations and those that have a more general acceptance in a given generation or cultural milieu. The former in a sense are merely pioneer. Certainly from a half to three-quarters of Sabian activity would never be regarded as particularly esoteric either by the occultist or his more conventional contemporary. It would be difficult indeed to push very far forward into the less recognized potentials of human capacity or understanding without taking full account of whatever normalities of life may be brought to special importance in the process, and by the same token it would be hard for a person of any sensitiveness to go through his days without an almost continual awareness of unidentifiable intangibles in his experience.

Modern occultism had its beginnings on the American scene with the new birth of Spiritualism in 1848, the establishment of Theosophy as an organized movement in 1875 and the rise of New Thought at about the turn of the century. Parallel European developments had roots penetrating back through the Middle Ages in what probably can be accepted as an actual and conscious continuity with the ancient world. The most important events in Europe leading to the present development of the arcane tradition have been the rise of speculative Freemasonry out of the craft guilds in England during the seventeenth century, the crucial modification of the age-old therapeutic or magical use of hypnotism by Mesmer in the eighteenth and the creation of psychoanalysis by Freud late in the nineteenth. The familiar name Rosicrucian was employed by mystic groups of Masons and subsequently by organizations of a more Theosophical nature, and at the present time there is an unending proliferation of labels. The facts of occultism's history are often garbled or obscured, and many are involved in hopeless controversy. A short history of the tradition, together with a summary of its teachings, are provided in the author's *Occult Philosophy*.

The arts and practices that have predominant recognition as occult are most importantly astrology, the cabala and the Tarot. An account of astrological history in terms of its literature is given in the author's *Astrology, How and Why It Works* (New York, Sabian Publishing Society, 1945). The cabala has widespread simplification under the more familiar designation of numerology, and an excellent and popular exposition is *Your Days Are Numbered,* by Florence Evylinn Campbell (Hollywood, Tora, 1931). In the first section of this manual it has been explained that the Sabian materials are completely cabalistic. Indeed, participation in the Sabian project is primarily an application of the cabala's basic principles to every department of everyday living. The Tarot is of world-wide interest in the arcane tradition but in Sabian procedures its use is restricted to the acolyte and legate disciplines.

The healing art has always been prominent in esoteric activity, but when it is taken in all its branches it is seen to be interwound inextricably with endless religious practices of both orthodox and heterodox nature. In its secular form it has become a myriad of therapeutic techniques, and except in some particular aspect under arcane auspices it can hardly be identified as occult. However, it is of primary significance in the Sabian project as one of the two main emphases, and so it will have considerable analysis in the pages to follow.

Eastern occultism is of importance equal to that of the arcane tradition of the Western world, and in consequence there is a parallel and necessary attention to the former in the Sabian inquiries. But consideration of any phase of the Oriental tradition remains an option for members of the group, primarily because the aspirant seeking the Solar discipline through the Assembly is usually oriented beyond much chance of modification to the ways and thought patterns of the West. In the East the division between the occult and nonoccult is psychological rather than intellectual, and is to be noted most readily in the apprentice system or unusually intimate relationship of the pupil or chela to his guru or teacher. This is a pattern of instruction with very ancient antecedents, and in the last two or three generations it has become familiar in the West through the unquestioning devotion demanded for the Masters by some of the esoteric societies. The intimacy is an age-old method for facilitating the oral and ultimately nonverbal communication on which high initiation is based, but in the Occidental world of today it is apt to be needlessly cumbersome. On the intellectual side of the Oriental contribution the discipline of the senses and prejudices is well represented by Yoga, and the transcendental speculation on the nature of man and the universe has its significant ordering in the Vedanta.

The Occult Literature

The literature of the esoteric tradition is voluminous beyond all belief, and there has been no adequate and impartial study of it as a whole. Ranging back into ancient times and into all languages, the books and manuscripts still in existence are scattered in libraries and private collections all over the world. Many writings that would be of the greatest value to the Sabian aspirant for collateral reading are out of print and difficult to find, and as a result he is restricted almost of necessity to the materials that are kept available for purchase or easy consultation by organizations whose particular beliefs and points of view are expounded and preserved. Thus the newcomer to occultism must gain a large part of the information with which he must work in a highly slanted or prejudiced form, learning only through his own experience how to screen out the worth-while from the fruitless and at times even from the ridiculous. Before he can proceed very far on any real path of aspiration he will have to know how to distinguish almost at first glance between what this author in his *Occult Philosophy* has found convenient to term the profane mysteries and the Lunar or Solar realizations lying beyond the outer façade.

Perhaps the most important work in modern and Western occultism is the *Secret Doctrine* by Helena Petrovna Blavatsky (London, Theosophical Publishing Society, 1888). With fascinating and on the whole remarkably convincing detail the text develops the conception of a sacred or literally esoteric all-knowledge screened carefully from the profane mind through all the ages, and now revealed to humanity by the special dispensation of divine hierarchies who have it in charge and indeed have been responsible for it through untold generations. The substance of this all-knowledge is presented in the framework of an evolution of the totality of existence through a series of orderly emanations. Involved are various planes of manifestation or worlds of expression on the spatial side, and on the temporal the great epochs to be recognized in (1) the formation and disintegration of planets and stars in the heavens, (2) the changes in the arrangement of the land masses relative to the waters on the surface of the globe and (3) the appearance and disappearance of the root races of man with their transient distribution in subraces and smaller units. The charting of all this is essentially mathematical. Reality is described as repetitive or cyclic, and in a sense spiral in motion, so that one cycle passes into another illimitably and all the smaller and larger components of anything in question are maintained thereby in a creative complementation.

Madame Blavatsky's work is not too difficult reading, and is both remarkable and illuminating in its wealth of reference. All the differentiations that measure and analyze the myriad outer appearances and activities of the objective universe, and that now are fairly familiar to the average person through geology, archeology, anthropology and similar sciences, are woven with infinite imagination into the great mathematical construct of the arcane tradition. And into this frame and with equal skill are then fitted the whole of the psychological and rational manifestation of conscious life, from man not only upward to all the evidences of divine beings but also down to the least recognizable aspects of living matter. The exposition is oddly haphazard, with a continual and merciless criticism of the science and philosophy as well as the religion of the nonoccultist, but the insights in their potentiality are superb. The formulation of them by Blavatsky and by those of the invisible fellowship on whom she draws is a monumental achievement by any standard of judgment.

The clearest simplification of this mathematical schematism, as it has come to an outstanding effectiveness in modern Theosophy, is unquestionably the *Rosicrucian Cosmo-Conception* by Max Heindel (Oceanside, Rosicrucian Fellowship, 1909). The most dramatic and stimulating capture of the emanation idea, as it has become the root of the best of modern Western occultism, is found in the *Outline of Occult Science* by Rudolf Steiner (in translation, Chicago, Rand McNally, 1914). Both these authors were Theosophists who became founders of their own organizations outside the Theosophical orbit. Both books start out with superlative clarity, and then thin out in divergencies of interest and emphasis that will be of little value to anyone reading them primarily for a general orientation.

In the *Enneads* of Plotinus (translation by Stephen Mackenna, London, Medici Society, 1921-30) the classical roots of the mathematical schematism on which the esoteric tradition rests can be examined in an earlier Western formulation. The exposition may not be easy reading for the aspirant, but it is of the utmost value in a contemplative perusal. Its author was born in Egypt in the third century and he brings a different and stimulating perspective to the divine emanations, and to man's interrelation with reality in its downward and upward aspects or its inward and outward potentials. Plotinus not only had an enormous impact on the early Christian church but in spirit if perhaps not in any literal succession of ideas he has provided much of the deeper foundation for various phases of the occult. This may be true particularly of modern New Thought and its dramatization of man's healing capacities. At times the beautiful prose rendering of the Greek by Mackenna is more a paraphrase than a translation, but it has preserved the original flavor and meaning with very real genius.

The development of the aspirant into his spiritual powers has a dramatization at the threshold of modern Western occultism in the novel *Zanoni* by Edward Bulwer-Lytton (London, 1842) and the fictional account of the cabalist's seeking in *The Comte de Gabalis* by Abbe N. de Montfaucon de Villars (Paris, 1670; translated with commentaries by Lotus Dudley, New York, Macoy, 1922).

The *Hidden Way Across the Threshold* by J. C. Street (Boston, Lee and Shepard, 1887) presents an excellent meditative approach to self-fulfillment. The hauntingly beautiful miscellany of insights and remembrances has come from a rich personal experience in the frame of modern Europeon occultism, and they have an essentially spiritualistic slant.

On the American scene the original *Science and Health with Key to the Scriptures* by Mary Baker Eddy (Boston, Christian Science Publishing Society, 1875) was an indigenous and unique development in the Western tradition. Truly epochal was the emphasis of man's self-creative potential as free from any necessary point of origin for its manifestation, that is, from any necessary control exercised by the time-and-space matrix of the workaday reality in which he finds himself. This insight provided the perfect complementation of Madame Blavatsky's revelation of man as nothing except the focus provided by his being for whatever elements may have a common convergence of effectiveness in his act or reaction. *In Tune with the Infinite* by Ralph Waldo Trine (New York, Crowell, 1897) is a simple and popular exposition of human nature in terms of this nothingness as it is brought to its something-ness through God's essential presence in its substance and in its powers of self-awareness and choice.

The aspirant entering the Sabian portal of the Solar Mysteries should read or at least examine these nine works of other than Sabian perspective or emphasis, or an equivalent number of others more or less of the same type and scope, during the course of his initial years under the discipline. This is recommended to the end that his realization may not be too conditioned by the points of view used as a basis for consistency in the Sabian materials.

The Invisible Fellowship

In addition to the written record of the occult tradition there is also the oral, or that which cannot take on the character of history or scientific report because on the one hand there is a lack of common and pertinent experience in which to anchor the communication and because on the other there is no possibility of normal verification for the facts involved. Thanks to its special nature the oral tradition has come to be known as occult knowledge. It frequently is unrealiable, since there are inescapable accretions or distortions from time to time, but its contribution may be very wonderful in view of its unlimited freedom from censorship at the hands of unimaginative and entrenched prejudice. The resurgence of Spiritualism in the past century has encouraged a flood of psychically derived materials, and has built up a superficial and spurious authority for the mass of unverified detail added to the unwritten account of arcane developments and their spiritual opportunity. The repetition of incidents and ideas of monotonous similarity has created a false sense of confidence in what the single mind obtains by way of psychic outreach through its unaided resources. Existing of their own weight the notions have pyramided themselves and exhibited the phenomenon common in creative fiction when a writer feels that his story actually is writing itself. All real discrimination is destroyed, and it becomes impossible to distinguish a symbolical from a literal significance. Myth comes to be taken very naïvely, or as an actual report of events. This development has hurt the truly valid claims of Western occultism for serious consideration in the modern world.

Under the Solar Mysteries there must be a ramification out into verifiable human experience in direct proportion to every inreaching participation in higher or essentially spiritual realization. Otherwise the consciousness will be quick to lose itself in its own disconnections or in the pyramiding of its illusions of the moment. For any genuine occult work there must be the ecclesia or assembly of the many for the sake of the growth and development of each one among them. It was in the light of this inescapable necessity that the Sabian ideal of the present generation had to become a group rather than an individual effort, once its author approached the limits of his personal outspread in gaining the needed verification of his esoteric insights. And by the same token the Sabian aspirant must work in quadrangles at the proper stage in his seeking, and must have a healing ministry or a task out in the world at the next point in his ultimate self-fulfillment. With this background of understanding it is possible to pick up an important thread of Solar Mystery orientation.

Once upon a time—as a fairy tale begins, and as any story should start if it comes from purely occult sources and in consequence lacks historical verification in any conventional sense—there was a congenial group of young priests who served the Memphite hierarchy in lower Egypt. In their generation an Atlantean occultism was widespread, not only across northern Africa but through the Mesopotamian lands where it was due to have a significant ripening and on over the Indus where it had met the gradual sweep westward of the emerging and vital masses of the new or Aryan root race. And it seems that these neophytes of the great temple had developed a taste for sitting at the river's edge and there discussing philosophical points. They were quite unaware of the fact that they were rushing in where the angels would fear to tread. Metaphysical speculation was a rarity at any point on the globe, possibly because the languages of some four or more millenniums before Christ did not facilitate anything of the sort. But in the fresh enthusiasm of their years they had become sensitive to a difficulty of the greatest psychological import. Indeed and in time they succeeded in making it articulate enough to interest some of their elders in their discussions, and to draw on the oral or nonverbal tradition which even then was far from inconsiderable in its resources.

For today's reader the matter necessarily must be put in words and forms of the late second millennium after Christ. Briefly they had come to realize that man is a generalizing animal perhaps above all else but yet lives his span so quickly, and comes to his end with so complete a cancellation of whatever substance or capacity of generalized realization he has built up within himself, that what should be his real nature has often had no chance to become any part of him at all. Superficially of course, and in every age, it is a commonplace for an individual to find himself facing death at just about the point when he has learned to live. And in the case of those equipped to serve their time and generation to an extent that may happen but once in a century or so it would appear a senseless waste. The younger participants in the talks at Memphis felt the challenge growing on them slowly. They felt a compulsion to do something about this.

To many it truly will seem a fairy tale that some six thousand years ago there was not even the slightest notion of any survival of personal consciousness after death, or for that matter the faintest conception whatsoever on any individual's part that he of and in himself actually was an entity in his own right. He was his family or his kind, and he acted in and of them at all points. In the languages then spoken there was no way to think or speak of an inner self as something discrete or as capable of any sort of introspection that people could know today. Concepts of things could not be put together creatively or imaginatively because there was no way of taking them apart in the mental operations to be found in Atlantis and its colonial expansion. There was a high civilization at times, but always as a class-structured edifice of services directed upward by what now would be identified as tyranny because it was in no way interested to share the least of rewards in a downgoing compassion. Many forces of nature and powers of the living organism were known and harnessed, but there was not the faintest flicker of the human ingenuity released when abstractions can be manipulated in their own context. Generalization did not begin with Atlantean experience, according to the occult tradition and its account of the evolution of the mind known to modern psychology. Instead it was a later Aryan light that brought the new realizations, and in the meanwhile made them possible in a sort of spiritual anticipation as the savage hordes of greater potential began to spill out of the Asian highlands.

As the oral tradition goes the young priests, in their free exchange of insights by the river, began to grapple with the vision of an individual survival and with the need of the race as a whole to have a better lot than the satisfaction of its animality or the cultivation of an intensified debauchery. It was beyond these Atlantean minds to realize that destiny must be the conscious creation of man if it is to be something that really can be said to be his, rather than something he merely suffers. But there was the sense of an unrealized and actually immortal potential. Therefore, as a step toward understanding the epochal project inaugurated at that time in the Nile valley, it may be well to bring the consideration back to the twentieth century and to an analysis of the four possible types of immortality.

First is the impersonal immortality carried to its uttermost. extreme in popular versions of Oriental philosophy. Everything is of the basic reality from which it has come through the universal emanation, and in time it will return to its origin in a completion of the cycle of its being. In man there is by this conception a divine spark around which his incarnations are formed and dissolved, and in final course the infinite speck of light that has established his existence will have rejoined the eternal flame. Meanwhile all that has participated in his experience has gone back to its own in similar fashion. Anything that can be said to be the individual in particular definition is transient and worthless in ultimate perspective. Hence it detaches itself and slips away quite properly, even as it has been gathered and held in possession in equally casual fashion. Man as taken in contrast with God is nothing, except in terms of what he derives from God, and at the end it is right that he should return it all to God and thereupon be fulfilled in his nothingness. The rewards of life come from an obedience to the negations by which all idea of good is surrendered to that splendid completeness of a total good in which only itself can share.

This point of view is the naïve recognition of self as uncompromisingly part and parcel of an all-self, and the rejection of every contrary notion as an invitation to the pain of not-belonging or to the pyramiding of bitter frustrations. With the individual who does not rationalize it philosophically it is the desire to surrender, or what is dramatized tellingly by Sigmund Freud in his later work under the figure of Thanatos in the Greek myths. In simplest manifestation it is craving for death or at least for exemption from further self-effort. It is the acceptance of end in an assimilation of personal completions to some total climax of reality. In a paradoxical sort of fashion it is the set of mind, relative to its own nature and continuity, that can be said to be the false rationalization of the earlier and mindless root races of man. In its more sophisticated aspect, as it survives into the epochs where mind comes into manifestation, it is that lean on the infinite regression in the thinking process against which a seeker under the Solar Mysteries is cautioned more than any other one fallacy. In everyday or practical life it is the wish of the individual to return to the womb, or to be assured in the possession of an essentially absolute security. In these aspects the conception does man a very great disservice, as should be obvious enough.

When seen as a constructive contribution to effective

self-realization the concept of impersonal immortality is the acceptance of a complete integrity for everything that is, thanks to everything's own act of continuity through the total cycle of its existence, and a consequent insistence on the all-important principle of *myob* or the minding of one's own business along with a rigorous determination to permit all else to mind its own as well. It is the power at the root of the passive resistance employed by Mahatma Gandhi and his followers to win India's independence, or of the sanction that all man-made law must have if it is to be enforceable. In the age and culture to which the young priests of Memphis belonged some six millenniums ago it was the prevailing if wholly subconscious realization of itself by human mentality. In its slow and over-all maturation the mind potential had yet to become individualized for any but the most exceptional person. In the terms of Sabian keywords the first of the four types of illimitable reality can perhaps best be described for to-day's purposes as the immortality of content or of substance.

The second of the four types is the biological immortality that alone had any actuality in human experience at the threshold of the present or Aryan root race. The conception has long been dramatized for all men through the ancestor worship found in the earliest roots of practically every religion. The veneration of the blood line is the first possible form of loyalty to the clan, and for ages the patriarchal society was the only successful form of organization for the human community. Sometimes the development was matriarchal, but whether with masculine or feminine dominance both privilege and obligation were seated in the inheritance. Selfhood was the genetic integrity that not only could demonstrate itself from infancy to senility but that also could offer a broader satisfaction for the instincts and passions demanding their expression without benefit of more than very rudimentary reasoning capacity. The fulfillment of the individual through the body's ability to reproduce itself was brought to particular historical emphasis in the Hebrew faith, in which the need for male issue to perpetuate the line led to such an idea as the levirate requirement that a man give a deceased brother a son by the proxy impregnation of the widow. Important to Christianity is the fact that out of the sense of a necessity for this continuity in the more personal elements of being, such as have created and preserved the family solidarity or tribal cohesiveness for so long, has come the identification of deity as a father in the over-all or ideal dimension of human well-being.

Nature worship, or the acceptance of the continuousness of life in the figure of a corresponding divine motherhood, has presented the same insight of the necessity that existence be cradled in continuity if there is to be any actuality of selfhood. On this side of the coin, however, the realization has turned to the extension of experience in spatial rather than temporal terms. As man could feel himself a participant in some pattern of relationship with the entities and objects surrounding him, even at a relatively mindless stage of evolution, he could act confidently in the business of being himself. The phenomenon is illustrated by children in parallel play, where rapprochement can be seen to develop through the operation of the imitative instinct. And yet it has not been until most recently that a Mary Baker Eddy could see with remarkable intuitive perception what Plato certainly had not been able to make clear more than two millenniums before, namely, that the mother principle is of the essence of God in an important fashion of its own. The idea involved at this point is simple, but none the less a difficulty because completely unfamiliar. Enunciated as a stark denial of reality to matter, it not only has outraged common sense but has made a false statement of itself.

A start toward understanding here is possible if it can be said that it is the embryo that establishes the womb in which it will be made manifest, as a literal fact no less true than the reverse relationship. Then perhaps the material world can be conceived as the handiwork of the Creator, not as He stands on the outside in a sense and commands it to come into being through a successiveness of cause and effect, but rather as a miracle of timeless co-operation with His creatures. The world's actual reality takes shape in an illimitable potentiality of itself as each of these creatures in its own absolute independence at core proceeds to dictate the nature of a personal milieu for its own particular outreaching. The general concordance so often mistaken for a cosmic order superimposed on the whole of creation from without thereupon is revealed as the godhead made manifest from within through the living or ever-adjusting matrix of the creativity available to all. It is Mother-God or nature as responsive to man beyond his fondest expectation, if he will but have it so. Deity thus becomes fulfillment as well as authority, and the distinction has little parallel to the division of labor represented by gender and seen in the superficial emphasis of matriarchal as in contrast with patriarchal. Man has long learned to know God through source and succession, and for long ages and through his ramification of experience in everyday vicissitudes he has learned also to recognize the powers of nature and perhaps indeed to worship them. But while he has grown to some achievement of spiritual liberation on the one side he has tended to cling to his bondage on the other.

The youthful Memphite priests of long ago would be fundamentally in sympathy with the biological immortality as a necessity for the health of a human society. They were close to the hieratic succession in the temple, and the authority of a superior who held office until death and ordained his successor with a laying on of hands. None the less their discussions at the river's edge had strengthened a realization that the transmission of a carefully preserved knowledge or wisdom individually from mind to mind as a spiritual birthright was an invitation to sterility of insight, and here again was a problem to be faced. Today an idle or pointless worship of the past has become a very obvious betrayal of the future. There are few who cannot realize that too great a dependence on established values and venerable symbols can cancel every quickening of life or actual realization of the present in its limitless opportunity and promise. Each man has a heritage that is ever the key to his character, and ever also a very rich endowment if only he brings it to account. This means a utilization of background, rather than any surrender to its compulsions. In consequence a fundamental requirement of the Solar Mysteries is the very genuine respect for personality, or an acceptance of the unimpeachable integrity of all personal roots in experience. The blood is the life, as the Hebrew scriptures explain with probably a very much more literal reference, and the line of life meanings and involvements the aspirant comes to treasure will be the measure of his illumination. In terms of the Sabian keywords there is here the immortality of the culture or of form.

The third of the four types is the social immortality that can be identified most usefully for the moment as the biological continuity of mind in the aspects of self-orientation and self-direction. According to a secular or materialistic point of view it is the ideal or rational order-ing of things. It has its most effective nonoccult dramati-zation in the idea popularized by Isaac Newton through his statement that whatever he achieved was a result of standing on the shoulders of giants who had gone before him. In giving a further instrumentation to the living power or actual continuance of previous and exceptional contributions to human knowledge and culture he was providing an example of the occult doctrine of reincarna-tion as this has its general acceptance in essence if not in terminology, that is, he was demonstrating the continuity of individual achievement within the matrix of society. Of importance to the aspirant at this point is not the possible cyclic rebirth of a given personality from time to time, but rather the continuance of any or every type of particular activity or accomplishment through which any conscious entity must express its existence to have any recognizable or discrete manifestation.

Obligation and opportunity become the twin facets of conscious existence, with personal survival a relatively minor issue for the moment. Here is the basis for the psychological insights of the occult tradition. Its complementary doctrines of karma and dharma are its promulgation of the principles involved, with the one defining man's social involvement and the other his fidelity to self-hood. They emphasize the fact that man must establish and adjust his relationships with his fellows continually and with unlimited modification, whether he is pleased to do this or not. The aspirant comes to know the necessities of his initiations-to-be through a continual perfecting of skills and understanding for the sake of those with whom he may have his everyday contacts. As he achieves the constancy or certainty of self-realization, such as in its ultimate manifestation is his eternal character or universal being, he is both creating the shoulders on which others may stand and learning to hold them erect and steady. Meanwhile there are evils in this emphasis on the inter-dependencies among men from the delusions of importance that come from a premature or incompetent assimilation to self of the achievements and merits of others on to the insensate lust for power by which an individual will seek to assimilate even more of other reputation or capacity to the structure of his own immediate being. Out of un-limited frustrations likely to develop will come need-lessly antisocial and perhaps even criminal acts with which every human society has to deal.

In the case of the young priests at Memphis toward the end of the Atlantean period it is probable that the ex-perience with the compatibility of temple life was respon-sible very largely for the development of their insights and for the remarkable depth of their thoughts. While with

all the warmth of their companionship in priestly dedication they had found no answer to the problem of a continuity in any personal consciousness beyond death they
yet, through their exchange of ideas, had become very
sensitive to the efficacy of a group awareness or of a continual sharing of realization. They had discovered that
the communication of the arcane knowledge need not be
all of one mind to another but instead could be of many
thinkers in close association. They also must have seen
that by working collectively to maintain the conscious insights they actually were creating a greater wisdom far
beyond the powers of formulation or comprehension possessed by any single individual. Here could have been the
seeds of modern scientific method, and very possibly the
historical beginning of what occultists usually term the
Great White Lodge. In any case there was a recognition
of procedures followed to this day by the Brothers in the
course of each of their incarnations. In terms of the
Sabian keywords what here is brought to spiritual significance is the immortality of the potential or of activity.

  The fourth of the four types is the personal immortality
that has remained a highly esoteric conception despite all
the efforts to explain it in everyday terms to long generations of spiritually-minded people. In consequence it has
been recognized principally in the form of widespread
and popular distortions. In Eastern religions and in much
superficial Western occultism a literalistic notion of reincarnation brings an individual back to earth in endless
life after life in a psychologically unchanging substance of
himself, putting on and taking off a vehicle of flesh as a
suit of clothes and ever suffering and causing others to

suffer as he somehow is transformed from something he is into perhaps a better something he is not. The unrealized fallacy is in failing to remember that what a person is will always be a continuance of his characteristic actions and reactions, and that for these there must be the essentially unbroken experience of acting and reacting in that particular continuity. The seductive analogy of sleep is not pertinent, any more than of a lacuna in attention, since in those cases no destruction of the organism is involved. A new body is not the same and obviously never could be the same as a sustainment for an experience to be picked up just where it was dropped on this most literal of levels. And of course and by the same token there is not even the remotest possibility of an equally necessary reproduction of the context of personal expression that has conditioned it and been conditioned by it in turn. Any actuality of ordinary memory surviving from a past life requires the successive circumstances to be exceptionally repetitive as in the case of a child's early return. For this phenomenon, however, there is some evidence of convincing order.

Christianity in general has escaped the difficulties arising with the acceptance of a literalistic chain of rebirths for the everyday personality by refusing to admit that anything of the kind is possible. Unhappily problems of an equal or greater sort have been raised with the conception of a soul not only created out of nothing at the threshold of embodiment but yet endowed most illogically at death with an on-going in the hypothetical reality of a nonphysical world. The line usually drawn between a first existence in a tangible organic form and a later one of wholly transcendental nature is an overemphasis of the Cartesian dualism of flesh and spirit, and similarly the common belief that existence framed in matter or in everyday time-and-space relationships is fundamentally evil is a survival of Gnostic ideas. Here of course is the old notion that whatever is remote or different is better. The farther pastures are the greener. And despite whatever anything may be, it should be something else. In consequence it often is assumed that man need not take too much responsibility for the inadequacies of daily life.

Personal immortality is acceptance rather than surrender, however, or is the phenomenon of selection by conscious choice as a transcendence of what otherwise would be either inevitable act under compulsion or uncontrolled reaction through conditioning. It is in no way a product of birth. Rather it involves a continuousness of rebirth or a constant choosing of the facets of reality from which to be born again and again in a growing complex of opportunity. Death has no sting because by the same token, and as a result of equally free choice, the individual is dying out of this and that whenever usefulness comes to an end or whenever fulfillment no longer has its signature in worthy works. The beginning in the body and the departure from the flesh, in a given span of focus among men on a physical level, progressively seem a minor punctuation in what has been coming to be of the major import. The person is less and less himself in the commonplace perspective as he becomes supremely what he is in the undying view of the initiate. Everyday life defines him in his own terms, and finds him blessed or not in the years of his incarnation, but to himself as he is quickened within himself the definition is through that which endures far more in other lives than his own. This is the implication of the Servant Songs in Isaiah, and the heart of Solar Mysteries discipline through all the generations.

The impersonal illimitability of the first type of immortality may now perhaps be seen to be no more than a dramatization of the basic integrity of existence. This cosmic integrity instruments the necessary degree of infinite regression through which all things may retract into their undifferentiated potentials whenever they are dismissed from conscious experience, and through which also everything needful for any experiencing entity from least to highest evolvement is ever at hand for its use when it is incarnate in a knowable reality. Meanwhile man as a creative manifestation of consciousness forever finds himself always at a center of evolution or self-emanation in the complex of embodiment serving him, and this is his biological immortality in terms of his character. And no less does he discover himself at the point of convergence in his interests and affairs that similarly marks his social immortality, or brings the total of his skills and functional capacities to significance in his relationships with his fellows. It is this many-faceted orientation of himself in selfhood that is cradled at a focus of convenience in time and space, and that is framed in the cosmic totality made understandable in the occult tradition through the mathematical interrelations charted so brilliantly by the periods and worlds, the races and vehicles and the related insights. As the aspirant makes the esoteric realizations his own he loses every inhibition that might hold him unnecessarily to the passions and impulses of an earlier or mindless humanity. His personality is immortal because through the proper management of himself and his world he can be what he wants to be, do what he wants to do, go where he wants to go and have what he wants to have. This is the popular affirmation of self-potential in the Sabian presentation of the Solar Mysteries. In terms of the Sabian keywords the bringing of all divine potentialities so uncompromisingly to a core in self is an immortality of consciousness or of the absolute.

Where then is ultimate reality in the occult tradition? It is where it always has been, right at hand ready either (1) to use with profit to self and everybody else or (2) to be permitted to administer limitation and frustration.

What then has the occult tradition done to truth? Nothing, except to show that the mind's expectation may embrace all experience in a greater understanding.

And is God still given His proper place in the consideration by the occultist? Certainly, since His works are seen only as they are in full accord with His nature, and since His nature after all is known by men only as the knowing eliminates every possible separation or destructive self-centeredness among them.

As the story of the Memphite priests goes, it was in their old age when the great insight came to them. With the dawning of the new light in their reasoning they quickened to what would be so very obvious in afterview. If men in actuality are what they do, as must be true of everything ultimately, were not their actions and reactions really of their inner consciousness rather than of their outer flesh and its mechanisms of sense and surface reasoning? And if an immortal inwardness could be made

possible in some fashion without the time-and-space embodiment and consequent fixities of orientation, would
that not be the answer to the inescapable waste of thought
and reflection that followed from the early cancellation of
outer personality or essentially sensual awareness through
physical death?

They had made the problem articulate through their
agony of speculation. Now they could ask if the association together in the exercise of a common and higher
realization could not somehow offer a species of substitute
embodiment. In a sense they had been experiencing this
very miracle of organic or creative communion in their
unbroken meetings, and at times it had seemed to them
that they were experiencing an aliveness of an initiate sort
or something singularly independent of the bodies in
which they held their individual focus of being. Within
the periphery of their unified aspiration they were strangely at one, and this atoneness might well become a new sort
of physical vehicle. It could be perpetuated if a dedicated
group of men such as themselves could undertake the task.
It then could serve any personality of high or illuminated
potentiality as a bridge from one incarnation to another.

With the recognition of the powers of a projective consciousness, whether in this or some other fashion, man
achieved the idea of vicarious atonement and so of vicarious attainment as well. Abraham would give perhaps the
first historical dramatization of the principle in its one
aspect when he discovered he could offer up the lamb in
lieu of his own son Isaac. Fifteen centuries or more later
the whole world would be taught that any person permit-
ting an unembodied and consciously immortal Jesus to

dwell within him would partake of the magic of God's ever-single or necessarily-of-one and so only begetting. Today the conventional and ecclesiastical emphasis still remains on the one side of the coin, and stresses salvation or affirms the gain to the individual who enters into the consciousness of the Saviour. The avatar himself, however, pointed out that the gathering together of two or three in his name, that is, in recognition of his act of living immortally as the archetypal divine offspring, was a condition of his presence and so by implication and as a matter of necessity the means through which his conscious or personal continuance was instrumented. In this and perhaps most simply can be seen the nature and function of the invisible fellowship described in the light of the oral tradition of certain of its origins long millenniums ago. In modern occultism it preserves a historical continuity of the great Lodge of initiates, and under the Sabian administration of the Solar Mysteries and thus in more immediate compass it is shared with the seeker. But he first of all must be willing to dedicate himself to facilitating the vicarious embodiment of the Great Ones in this manner, as need and opportunity arise, and also and in doing so he must aspire to an ultimate and enduring contribution for which he may require such a service in turn.

The Arcane Instruction

Man's thoughts require language, and its symbols rise from the material and tangible living that begins for him with his birth and that has been and will continue to be anchored in the collective potentialities of all men. The thinking process is the very essence of power and self-fulfillment, and in consequence an unchanging truth to be recognized through the mind is conceived as that which in its gaining might well elevate man to God's stature. In the old myths it was necessary for divine intelligence to head off the ambitious human creature when there seemed a likelihood he would eat of the forbidden tree of knowledge in the Garden of Eden, or when he made his great challenge in the erection of the Tower of Babel. Actually, with his foundation in solid experience, there is no limit to the heights the seeker may reach.

The occult tradition has met the rational aspiration of mankind, arising as the root races evolved beyond their mindless beginnings, with the conception of an Eternal Wisdom. The functional if hardly literal changelessness of this is dramatized rather commonly by designating it the ancient wisdom and identifying its roots in early human speculation, or in a time when the mind's insights were not handicapped by the greater sophistication of later cultures. Moreover the backward view is able to maintain a better perspective, thanks to the remoteness of the prejudices and unessential side issues characterizing the prior ages during which the ideas were given their initial formulation. What is preserved for mankind in this fashion, whether in written or oral form, is not a body of information in any usual sense. It is not a compilation of principles and details of technical instruction such as can be gained through a process of attention and retained in memory through the language in which they are expressed. The words it is necessary to use are always involved too intimately in various segments of the culture with all the momentary or shifting distortions, and in consequence through the millenniums the arcane instruction has been not so much a proposition of verbal exposition as of a curious sort of incidental illustration.

With the development of the Solar Mysteries the Eternal Wisdom has been presented to the aspirant as primarily something in which he participates, and this not only is the mode of expression employed in the wording of the Sabian neophyte pledge but is the essence of the apparently haphazard way in which he is asked to browse through the lesson materials at the start of his Sabian affiliation. By participation is meant a contribution of knowing in equal measure to what is gained by way of occult insights. The content by which principles are given flesh and life is supplied by the seeker. The arcane knowledge is that which at all times is expanded beyond the delimitations of a time-and-space or physical world, and hence and also that which only in some literal context will have the definite substance or sharp statement of the sort demanded in modern education. When esoteric realizations are all dressed up with the trappings of erudition, or are crowded into neat formulas of magical pretense for a popular appeal, they are at once frozen into the crystallizations of the culture. Their broader scope or enduring reliability is lost, and occultism itself loses repute. What the aspirant gains ultimately under the Solar Mysteries is not a great mass of restricted information but rather a facility for manipulating or directing the components of experience. He is equipped to produce results precisely as he envisions them, and to apply the least of his efforts to worth-while end. Most simply the concern is with method as perfected through a discipline of mind or the process of initiation.

Arcane instruction in consequence cannot encourage

any overbalanced attention to ideas, or the rational side of man's nature. Under Sabian auspices it is presented as at root the cabala, and in the great tradition a cabalistic competency is said to require the perfect mating of poetry and philosophy as such was exemplified in the life and works of Ibn Gabirol. Madame Blavatsky has given early and important testimony to the unique role of this eleventh-century thinker in the rise of Western occultism, and it is on his formulations that the Sabian project has put its more individual foundations. He ranks high among the world's poets, and in the light of his example the Sabian rituals have been given a basic lyrical emphasis through the wide variety of verse form employed. His *Fons Vitae* or *Source of Life* is coming to have increasing academic recognition for its contribution to general philosophy. His centralization of reality at the core of experience, making it ever a construct of the process of being, is the key to the whole shaping and refinement of Sabian realizations. In view of the cabalistic necessity the aspirant is asked to culture his capacity both to produce and to appreciate beauty in parallel to his development of the power of clear thinking.

The Sabian lessons are intricately cabalistic in the sense that their contents are ordered and their presentation tempered to cultivate a creative complementation of heart and head, or a blending of the senses and the reason into each other. Thus a student at length may become a true participant in the Eternal Wisdom. The newcomer, however, may be in a hurry to get to the goal, and thereupon find the materials hard beyond all endurance. Hence he has to be told that this follows only when he fails to

employ them as directed, that is, from the start seeking an
experience that builds on his own psychological resources.
It is essential that he realize the real adventure of his quest
very early, and thereby begin to catch the dramatic overtones of the ideas with which he has now begun to work.
These are of the magic of the poetry, and a sensitiveness
to them is strengthened through the rituals.

The general presentation of the Sabian materials follows two major modes of approach to the arcane knowledge. Both of these have been characteristic of the
occult tradition through the ages, and not only are they
equally effective but each provides an enlightening demonstration of the values to be found in the other. The first
and most common of the procedures is the uncovering of
hidden meanings and implications in the sacred texts and
secular classics of the world. Writings that have come out
of high inspiration and often exceptional genius at the
beginning, and that have been preserved and usually re-
worked from time to time with at least an equivalent skill
and appreciation as they gain a response from human
hearts and minds over the generations and centuries, tend
to establish themselves as an articulation of the racial
mind. Thus they offer a means for rehearsing the venerable experience, or participating in the overtones of esoteric realization, in a way quite impossible through any
mere verbal communication. A large part of the some
three thousand Sabian lessons expound and illustrate
the procedure. They provide the aspirant with an im-
mense breadth of application, and so every chance for a
personal quickening unconditioned by the current prejudices. His orientation is in a span of many millenniums.

The second and parallel approach to the Eternal Wisdom in a modern Western occultism is more on the spatial side, and is a participation in the process through which the sacred scriptures and secular classics have an origin in the first place. In the less common instance it is wholly original authorship, such as can have valid recognition only in long afterview, but for the major part it is a contemporary reworking of texts for a better or more convenient dramatization of meanings and implications. The reclothing of insights in a vernacular tongue helps facilitate a deepened present experience with the enduring realizations that actually constitute the racial mind. It gives a dramatic immediacy of understanding that perhaps is not achieved as easily through the writings of more established historical roots. Thus in possible substitution for the Jewish and Christian Bibles, the Koran or the Bhagavad-Gita and other scriptures of the East there are the Life of Apollonius of Tyana by Flavius Philostratus out of the Roman world (in translation, New York, Putnam, 1912), the Book of Mormon (Salt Lake City, Church of Jesus Christ of Latter-Day Saints, 1830), the Oahspe compilation of John Balloe Newbrough (Los Angeles, Kosmon Press, 1882), the Aquarian Gospel of Jesus Christ by Levi H. Dowling (Los Angeles, Leo W. Dowling, 1907), and on beyond any practical enumeration. A complete recasting of New Testament account is found in such a gem of insight as *The Apocalypse Unsealed* by James M. Pryse (New York, John M. Pryse, 1910).

The approach has been employed in the Sabian work, producing what has been designated conveniently as a recension of text, in the case of the 82d Psalm, chapter 44 of

Isaiah and chapters 1-3 of Ezekiel. The paraphrased sections were needed for the rituals, and they will be found in the latter pages of this manual. On a larger scale in the Sabian project is the interpretation of the entire book of Daniel as a preservation in masked form of a traditional Chaldean Book of Initiation, and a complete paraphrase of the whole illustrates the hypothesis.

The Arcane Dedication

Immortality consists of a living without beginning or end, and in consequence it is necessary for the individual aspirant (1) to establish the roots of his personal awareness anciently enough in the evolution of the race to endow himself with the stature he needs for his aspiration and (2) to project the branches of his faith far enough into the future to fulfill all possibilities of divine consummation. By the same token the Sabian Assembly in undertaking to sustain the initiatory progress of the seeker must activate (1) an unbroken continuity of group consciousness from a phase of human experience back sufficiently in racial development to embrace the beginnings of all who may seek unfoldment under its auspices and (2) an uncompromising or total and impartial respect for every possible aspect of man's self-expression now to be found or yet to be made manifest. Because the initiate-to-be and his invisible fellowship must serve each other equally and in an identity of creative potential if the Sabian project as a whole is to have any spiritual actuality, or is to remain a valid initiatory body under the Solar Mysteries, the tie to original source must be ever beyond question. Obviously any attempt to locate this too definitely in objective global history would be defeated through its literalism. What constitutes eternity is not so much the absence of beginnings and endings as a creative and free sustainment in what is both prior and subsequent adequately for a given manifestation. Eternal reality provides a functional zero in duration, or a practical comprisement in successiveness from which time never needs to be projected in either direction. Here is the proposition kept simple in general occultism by presenting all ultimates of progress as circular or cyclic. And also and by the same token the concept of absolute integrity as poise at the core of itself involves the parallel convergence or convenience of all-potentiality in space relations. The term in the esoteric tradition for this point of unimpeachable reference in which any given manifestation has its dynamic self-impetus under any and all possibilities of existence, with never a relationship that can be conceived behind or beyond it in any sense, is laya center and it has been given preliminary description in the opening section of this manual.

The concept actually identifies no more than the illimitability of interweaving realities throughout all existence, but it is this phenomenon of spiritual independences in mutual sustainment that constitutes the higher or one-and-only reality forever eluding language. Thus the initiate increasingly becomes a laya center for the new and truly eternal destiny of himself, as well as of all with whom he may share its inner and absolute stability, and the invisible fellowship of the Sabian project and of the Lodge by which it is chartered is a laya center of which these others are all a special manifestation without in any way compromising their identity or its own. In lesser outer

dimension but fully a part of the whole in an equal absoluteness are the projects of all the workers in the occult
tradition. As each of these develops a characteristic task
of spiritual potentiality, in which he may fulfill himself,
he constitutes himself a laya center for the eternal contribution through its accomplishment. The foundation
of all Sabian work in consciousness is effort directed to
the spiritual sustainment of the vision in its various details, and this means the maintaining and strengthening
of these superficially mysterious zero functions through a
continuous rehearsal of the differentiations of experience for which they serve as causeless origin. In Sabian
usage the term is not restricted to primeval points of
source, since an absoluteness of beginning is recognized as
the basis of all true choice. The fact that this absolute of
self-act may be found in the smallest or most immediate
context no less than in one of immeasurable remoteness
reveals the spiritual source at the core of everything.

A life elevated to the level of avatars and adepts becomes more the laya center of a group reality than the
individual of immortal personality that establishes and
strengthens it from incarnation to incarnation. It develops the outer poise and universality of realization characterizing the great souls everywhere. In time there may
be uncounted millions who will find a peace and an enlightenment for themselves by dwelling within its potentiality, and in this they may gain the salvation promised
by most religion. To varying degrees the less evolved
seeker becomes a species of incarnation of the more exalted
one, and thus helps provide the illuminated server with
the vicarious embodiment he can use in his higher self-

ьustainment for performing the tasks to which he is dedicated. The faithful are saved because they are enabled
to live an eternal plussage of selfhood, and in doing so
to help others to do as much in turn. And under the
Solar Mysteries this is fellowship rather than a hierarchy.

The Masters or Brothers are men who have developed
and held an immortality by a continuous maintenance of
conscious personality, quite apart from the fleshy embodiment of their regular incarnations, and in this unbroken
chain of unending activity or service they have created
the primary laya center of occult vision and effort through
which the great Lodge continues in its effective existence.
In their various normal lives during recent millenniums
these individuals have proved their inherent stature by
the achievements or contributions of weight sufficient to
sustain the tradition in its outer manifestation, and each
of them on the inward and eternal side is the creator and
sustainment of some special laya center by which his own
consciousness keeps its identity. Twelve of these long-
experienced initiates serve as the invisible and administrative council of the Sabian Assembly, and ten of them are
associated with the vision permanently and have been for
generations. The other two are revolving members of
the circle, but for simplicity's sake they are given fixed
identification in the Sabian system of letters, that is, each
letter in these two cases referring to a different individuality at different times. Three of the total group are identified, as in Theosophy, as *H*, *K* and *M*. For the others
A, *B*, *C*, *D*, *E*, *F*, *G*, *J* and *L* are assigned quite arbitrarily.

In Sabian practice all personal information about the
Masters is restricted along the lines already explained, and

whatever literalistic detail may be needed at times is provided in the oral work on the legate level. As pointed out it is not the individual who is likely to have any significance to the Sabian aspirant, but rather the laya center that actually represents his participation in the common vision. In order to help each seeker get the ever-intangible feel of the fundamental zero points of creativity constituting the general project, as these represent a basic division of labor established by the Great Ones in sponsoring the Assembly, all lesson material and rituals or other details of the procedure are given letters of imprimatur to identify the one of the twelve with whom the author has worked consciously and particularly in preparation or research. What may be a further aid for this sort of intuitive outreach is that since October, 1934, all Sabian effort has been patterned in aspects of function or group ordering known as the Twelve Plans.

THE TWELVE PLANS
The Structure Of The Assembly

L: THE DISCIPLINE   A Grecian-style initiation provided by study and activity in neophyte, acolyte and legate grades of individual accomplishment.

C: THE LAYA CENTERS   The maintenance of the Assembly as a network of active autonomous groups, each a matrix of race, culture or personal distinctiveness.

D: THE MONITORS   The strengthening of continuity for the laya centers through the oversight of their functions by the immortal leadership they develop.

H: THE SCREEN OF PROPHECY   The editing and reissuing of the Sabian lessons and letters in their cycles and so building a creative rapport with current history.

The Orientations of The Assembly

E: SPIRITUALISM   The doctrine of personal immortality dramatized by the contribution of the deceased to the living through psychic or like phenomena.

F: THE CABALA   The doctrines of occult cosmogony and psychology dramatizing a superior reality in which man may gain exceptional gifts and powers.

A: ASTROLOGY   The doctrine of interlacing relevancies that dramatize a cosmic order through which man can master everyday life and control his destiny.

G: MENTAL THERAPY   The doctrine of mind discipline or soul quickening dramatized in meditation or self-assertion and conscious rejection of limitations.

The Techniques of The Assembly

M: METAPHYSICS   The way of ordering life by a world view in philosophy or an account of reality well justified in history and verified through faith.

J: EDUCATION   The way of ordering life by training people in appreciation of common values or in adjustment to realities of broadest acceptance.

B: DRAMA   The way of ordering life by exaggeration of its features in order to bring dignity to man's activity and build enduring rapport in human ties.

K: ART   The way of ordering life by exalting special elements of it sufficiently to add dimension to realization and so develop aesthetic appreciation.

The Work in Consciousness

Work in consciousness is generally known in the arcane tradition as meditation or concentration. In essence it is a conscious direction and maintenance of attention until some selected and creative phase of interest becomes an underlay in all other awareness of (1) the self and (2) the world of immediate pertinence. When the achievement of this for the meditative period is repeated at relatively regular intervals over a considerable period of time the result can be an establishing or strengthening of a laya center that will have the power not only (1) to sustain real and persisting effort of a desired sort but (2) to pre-cipitate the needed convergence and co-operation of all vital concomitants. In even the least use of this discipline of consciousness an individual may build morale and re-fine his inherent integrity beyond all expectations. The operation of man's basic predilections along these lines is dramatized by the inner censor of the mind when the subject under the superficial control of another intelli-gence in hypnotism will refuse to accept or act on any idea that runs counter to his underlying scruples. Because of the strength of this inner set of temperament the de-velopment of a moral inviolability, usually in special alignment with some definite ideal, has long been the major goal of all genuine occult initiation.

In the nonoccult world it is of course a commonplace for individuals to steel themselves to their purposes through a continual and conscious entertainment of their devotion to their own ambitions. On the destructive side there is no difference in effectiveness when the loyalty to ends is a lust for supremacy among others, or is an isola-tion of the self from them in a debasement of values and an acceptance of the false exaltations leading to megalo-mania and hopeless delusions. In the happier case of the great mystics the desired achievement is an ever-closer communion with divine intelligence, and implicit in their effort is a sharing of God's potential with the whole of God's creation. This is the practice of the presence as the continual rehearsal of every inner heightening of spirit, and at its best it has its frame in an uncompromising love and respect for mankind. The inescapable contribution of beauty and understanding that results has provided some of the richest episodes in man's spiritual history.

The bringing of God into partnership with the self in the purely religious meditation is of course the best of all correctives against destructive ideas of self-importance. And on the other side of the coin it is the mystical way that endows religion with its genuine depth. Hence it makes no difference whether the self's outreaching under a transcendental orientation takes the form of (1) prayer and supplication in the most conventional sense, (2) a more reflective contemplation of the enhanced presence of the divine in human affairs as a consequence of ordered devotions of a more occult sort or (3) sheer self-release in the momentary but repetitive ecstasy of approach to higher reality known to the mystic at hallowed times and in sacred places and always characteristic of high initiation. Communion with eternal intelligence through some form of meditation, in the largest or over-all sense, is the entire substance and actuality of worship. Ritual becomes important as the formalized rehearsal of the meditative experience.

Meditation under the Solar Mysteries may embrace every sort of inner wrestling of the soul with itself, in an effort to achieve an eternal reconciliation with an absoluteness centered in the godhead, but it has its most worthy concern with the aspirant's service to others and his self-service in preparation for the role he would play as the server. Thus the directing of interest must be practical or quickened by human need in some respect, and the attempt to achieve a purely negative receptiveness or a supposed opening of the inner being to higher inspiration without personal self-expenditure will prove an inevitable delusion. To enter the silence properly cannot mean accepting an emptiness as some sort of a greater reality, within which to wait on the caprice of a power actually external to the self as far as any familiarity with it is concerned, but instead is an effort to bring self to center sufficiently to avoid all distractions and disconnections and thus to facilitate its true mystical or more ultimate experience of itself. What is never to be desired is the artificial concentration of consciousness such as seeks to exclude all extraneous elements through its rigidity, or through the strength of the will sustaining it. There must be instead the fluidity of an awareness that is able to wander here, there and everywhere without ever the underlying self-direction changing or wavering in the least degree. Useful in this connection is the retrospection exercise just before going to sleep, and its review of the events of the day beginning with the last and working backwards to morning while giving each an evaluation in the light of the ideals held and goals sought in the course of all the trivialities.

The meditation period may well be ritualized. In the Sabian Assembly, and formally, this means participating in the healing ceremony with others or conducting the ceremony privately. Informally it is the quiet time of not

too protracted duration repeated at scheduled hours on certain days or everyday. Devotional reading, music and the
like may be employed with advantage to set the mood of
the meditative self-orientation. The postures, breathing exercises and contemplation of the body's chakric centers in
Eastern occultism may be adopted profitably by seekers
in the West for whom they have special appeal. For the
use of aspirants who find it helpful an identification of the
invisible sponsor with whom a cycle of special affinity
may possibly be indicated is issued to every member of
the Assembly monthly. The meditation letter so provided
may suggest, through its correspondence with the im-
primaturs of the various materials and rituals, the special
possibilities of inspiration through a turn to these at the
times of private devotions. Where there are special needs
or problems the use of healing slips may be helpful, and
the nature of these is explained in connection with the
healing regimen.

When meditation is employed in furthering the healing
for others the aspirant undertaking this, whether as (1) an
individual acting on a request made to him privately or
(2) a professional healer or (3) a member of the Assembly assigned to this service, makes his touch with the
consciousness of the person in distress by employing some
one of the numberless techniques long established in the
esoteric tradition. The first group of these therapeutic
measures comprises the more objective methods usually
designated as occult. In Spiritualistic practice the medium
with or without supplementary procedures such as the
laying on of hands will take on the condition, as Spiritual-
ists explain the matter, and use the recuperative or re-

generative powers of his own organism as heightened in trance or otherwise to eliminate the destructive factors. Somewhat similar is the procedure coming down through medieval alchemy when discarnate entities or occultists volunteering for the self-projection of their energies during sleep are enlisted for ameliorative manipulations by a species of materialization at a point of need, or when subhuman nature spirits are put to work in this fashion, and such efforts are directed to those requesting help by an act of will during the meditative period. Many occult groups depend on their invisible workers, or highly evolved souls and perhaps even the Masters in special cases, to perform this sort of service. It is a widespread practice to facilitate the direction of the healing help by laying out the healing slips or letters of request in a special place set aside for the purpose, and in particular to do so during the night hours.

Quite distinct from the therapeutic methods generally classified as occult is the more strictly mental type of healing identified in the Sabian materials as New Thought. This technique involves taking the sick or troubled individual in mind and seeking, through a rapport in consciousness and by a contemplative reflection, to bring him back to balance in his own psychological and corresponding physiological integration. The assistance of divine agency is nearly always invoked for the success of this essentially spiritual reordering, and in all such cases an acceptance of a particular metaphysical or theological point of view is required from the person to be helped. Indeed, such acceptance usually is necessary for the rapport of minds from which any results must follow. In this area the holding of a proper form of belief is often presented as able of itself to cure virtually all ills of body, mind or personal affairs.

There is a logical difficulty in the part God is seen to play in any and all healing. Sooner or later there is the question why He permits an illness in the first place if He is willing to remove it when asked to do so. Certainly unacceptable is the notion of a deity who withholds His love except when those on the inside track, through knowing what to do, are able to bring it into manifestation. God cannot be God if the control of His operations is not to be vested wholly in Himself. Actually of course the problem has been created by the superficialities of human rationalization. Everything in which man is involved is a proposition of experience or consciousness at root, and illness no less than health is something experienced and real only in that fact. It is in every individual's power to alter his experiencing pattern more or less at will, and as he has a change of heart or desire his situation follows along in train. The idea is not that God is anything apart from the unprofitable activities of the particular person but that anyone in trouble is apt to ask a participation of divinity in his affairs, even when not at all inclined to do so during the times they go well. Man generally is willing to function in a larger dimension when the smaller one refuses to support the destructive aplomb in which he has been resting content.

The Sabian healing ministry is centered in the healing meeting, and in the therapy carried on by special meditation quadrangles for those who ask to be placed on the healing list. The need for help is seen as a lack of balance or of proper poise in experience, that is, as a deficiency of the personal laya center. Each individual is helped as he is brought through the meditative rapport into the great pool of consciousness constituting the laya center for the project as a whole. The functions of nature always tend to restore themselves when their sustaining or underlying integrity has an adequate reserve of its own potentials, together with a properly creative capacity for self-mobilization in an emergency. Divinity is touched as the being is kept in fluid equilibrium at center, and the touch is lost in the sense of separation or of missing the mark that was the actual conception of sin at the beginning of the great Hebraic-Christian line of prophecy. Thus healing is a return to God in quite practical fact, and it is the way of the heart that reveals this to mankind.

Summary

The broad orientation of the Sabian project is in the tradition known as occult, arcane or esoteric. This is an area of human understanding that embraces the supernatural and all speculative approach to the unknown, and of special importance are the ways of self-dedication and discipline known as initiation. The goal is to develop the unsuspected powers of man, and to help him direct them to the improvement of himself and his world.

Modern occultism had its American beginnings with the new birth of Spiritualism in 1848, the founding of the Theosophical Society in 1875 and the rise of New Thought at the turn of the century. The events of parallel importance in Europe were the emergence of speculative Freemasonry in the seventeenth century, the redevelopment of hypnotism by Mesmer in the eighteenth and the creation of psychoanalysis by Freud late in the nineteenth.

The esoteric arts and practices given a primary significance are astrology, the cabala and the Tarot. Healing is even more important, but only certain of the therapeutic techniques can be identified as essentially esoteric. Eastern ideas and methods are significant and effective but not always practical in a Western milieu.

Out of an occult literature that is voluminous beyond belief, and as supplementary to the Sabian books and materials, the *Secret Doctrine* of Blavatsky, the *Rosicrucian Cosmo-Conception* by Heindel, the *Outline of Occult Science* by Steiner and the *Enneads* of Plotinus present the mathematical ordering of reality that is a fundamental characteristic of esoteric thinking. The novel *Zanoni* by Bulwer-Lytton, the *Comte de Gabalis* by de Villars and the *Hidden Way Across the Threshold* by Street offer valuable dramatization of initiation, and *Science and Health with Key to the Scriptures* by Eddy and *In Tune with the Infinite* by Trine give the original flavor of mental healing in the New World.

The invisible fellowship is the designation for a group type of knowing or realization of experience where ordinary language does not transmit meanings adequately, and it is represented by a supernatural lore that usually has been communicated in secret from teacher to pupil and that otherwise is conveyed psychically and in consequence distorted easily and at times rendered quite unreliable. Out of this occult lore comes the account of a number of young priests who became interested in the problems of human immortality some six millenniums ago, and who perhaps first laid a foundation for the Great White Lodge.

There are four types of immortality. Impersonal immortality is represented by the conception of emanations, with reality in each or any of its phases emerging from a transcendent perfection and then returning to its source after the sojourn in time and space. This is a primary concept in Eastern philosophy and is important in the Sabian project because it affirms the essential integrity of everything-that-is and so dramatizes the necessity of *myob* or a minding of one's own business by every component of the universal whole.

Biological immortality is represented by the ancient Hebrew stress on the importance of male heirs, or of a continuity of man preserved in a succession of offspring. Primitive religion gained much of its power through the veneration of ancestors. Nature worship developed an appreciation for a divine principle of endless bounty, and this insight has been the basis of modern New Thought. This type of immortal continuance is to be seen in the successorship of initiates.

Social immortality is the enduring of human achievements as men take the torch from each other and continue in the race forward to a better opportunity in a better world. It is with this emphasis on a significant being-in-doing that the invisible fellowship becomes an actuality, and that the occult conceptions of dharma and karma have their proper instrumentation.

With personal immortality comes real appreciation of the doctrine of reincarnation, and of the necessity to preserve man's consciousness from life to life in order to avoid an almost complete waste of his self-perfecting during each incarnate span. The realization of a possible substitute embodiment makes it possible to conceive of a vicarious atonement as a basis for a higher religious development in the present race, and of a vicarious attainment as a mode of a practical and more personal accomplishment without any surrender to the limitations of time and space.

The Eternal Wisdom is not so much a knowing as a continual participation in the immortal potentials of all things, and Sabian procedures are shaped to make this clear in all possible ramification of detail. Everything is ordered on a cabalistic pattern to facilitate the realization, and what this means most fundamentally is a bringing of poetry into balance with reason. As an aid to higher understanding the great religious scriptures and secular classics of the world are given special interpretation, introducing the seeker to the progressive levels of meaning to be found, and fresh materials of greater deviation from the conventional are made available or actually created to help him in his recognition of the arcane patterning.

The laya center as the zero point of potentiality to be found lying at the foundation of any and all experience, and located deeply enough and ramifying broadly enough to vivify illimitable possibilities in any conceivable case, is seen to be the fact of source for that consciousness of which all things are taken to be the ultimate manifestation. The aspirant is shown how he may instrument his dedication in terms of laya center. The Master is revealed as an individual who has developed to the point where his continuity of lives has identified itself with a laya center of importance to the persons and objectives he must serve as a condition of his initiation, and the Sabian project gains its organic structure through particularities of its potentials that can be associated in each specific instance with the Masters who constitute its council. Thus these Great Ones can be identified most effectively for each seeker by the twelve plans in and through some one or more of which he will be able to understand his part in the Sabian vision.

The work in consciousness is the heart of the Sabian project, and the healing ministry its strength. Meditation in essence is the conscious direction and maintenance of attention until some selected and creative phase of interest becomes an underlay in all other concern, and there are innumerable and perhaps equally acceptable ways for achieving the desired morale or strengthened integrity of self and others. Healing is the use of widely varying techniques for strengthening the regenerative powers of the individual organism, or revivifying the point of creative poise in some area of experience. At root the process is a conscious return to God.

THE SABIAN PROCEDURES

The essence of occult procedure is an ordered experience with all the higher potentialities of human nature. In the Sabian Assembly the rituals and meditative practices employed to this end are little different from ceremonies and functions found commonly in everyday life, but the method of discipline or illumination of the mind is wholly esoteric. The work in consciousness and the individual aspirant's faithfulness to the rhythm and substance of his dedication are the strength of the project, but the study of the materials is the foundation of any achievement whether this happens to be a personal contribution or a collective advancement. Attention already has been given to the nature of arcane instruction, and now consideration must turn to the group rehearsals that in a sense create and preserve the Eternal Wisdom. The approach to reality in any such rehearsal has the sanction of untold centuries, and indeed has been illustrated in the riverside discussions of the young Memphite priests of the oral tradition now first brought to written account. And since 1947 there has been the new-found contemporary evidence of the practice in the Qumran community near the Dead Sea some two millenniums ago, in connection with the Hebrew Torah. The details can be deduced with every logical certainty from the manual of discipline discovered in the nearby caves, as well as from the parallel **Zadokite**

Document turning up at Old Cairo in 1896-7 but not then appreciated in its import.

It was the practice of these presumably Essene monastics to divide their members into three shifts, for a study of the law twenty-four hours around the clock every day of the year including the Sabbath. The Qumran brotherhood was an interesting fruitage of the Hasidic movement that had its most objective survival in the Pharisees, but that probably developed its greater inner power and enduring influence in the more secret or esoteric groups such as the one now brought to prominence through the Dead Sea Scrolls. By study of the law was meant not an intellectual acquisition of its content, but rather a repeated experience of its significance through what in modern times would be termed an open discussion. It was a continual exchange of views and insights as those taking part grew in comprehension, and so gave the ideas their transcendental character by sharing them under these special circumstances. In quite literal fact each of these ancient seekers was becoming a conscious participant in the Eternal Wisdom, as the goal of initiation is expressed in the Sabian neophyte pledge. Thus it can be understood why the new member of the monastic company, according to their manual of discipline, was required to contribute not only his worldly means but also his wisdom. He was expected to dedicate his capacity to share his spiritual realizations. The sharing from Sabian perspective can be seen not only facilitating a personal immortality but also helping maintain the invisible fellowship through which the great Lodge had come into existence.

Since the rehearsal of this sort is never primarily of the

words or the particularity of statement in which the ancient record is to be found preserved in any given age or culture, but rather always is a matter of a higher experience continually revivified through a fresh and individual adventure into its potentialities for each participant in the process, the Sabian project cannot be said to be intellectual in any over-all sense. There ever will be those among the aspirants who will choose to perfect themselves in areas the world would consider erudite, but this is merely one of many options available for the particular temperament. The rehearsal is of the reality that survives time and space in the form of ideas, and so is of the mind truly enough, but it need not be of the least complexity for that seeker who does not have the opportunity or perhaps the desire to develop the exacting skills of erudition. His service should be as great, and his rewards are merely different. In any immortal perspective there can be neither a more nor a less. And what possibly could be a basis of comparison among seekers in any dimension of eternal orientation?

The Sabian Lessons

It has been explained that the Sabian materials are cabalistic in the ordering of content, in the use of words and in the structure of each sentence and paragraph. They are not to be approached primarily as a source of information but rather as a basis for the particular type of experience needed for participation in the Eternal Wisdom. As a means for providing the necessary spread of this in a time-and-space reality, nearly all the lessons have been prepared in the guise of commentary on the best known and most available contributions of philosophy and religion to man's understanding in the Western world where the Sabian project has its present and convenient roots. There are some strictly occult expositions, as in the astrological presentation and the refinement of the magic squares of idea. Much attention is given to the universal symbolism to be found in such nontechnical and nonspiritual literature as the household tales of the Grimm brothers, to which reference has been made. Each lesson runs to about twelve hundred words, and all are issued in mimeographed form. The titles of the various series, with the letter imprimatur and starting dates of issue and reissue, are listed in the appendix.

All active members of the Sabian Assembly receive two basic lessons each week. One is on the Bible, and the other is on philosophy for the first half of the Sabian year and on some phase of symbolism or less technical material for the other half. There are enough lessons in each of these principal categories to constitute a cycle of somewhat less and of somewhat more than twenty years respectively, and no beginning or end is involved in either case. The continuous issue in regular order brings different considerations together in each repetition of the cycles. The convergence of these particular expositions, as well as of accompanying other materials either in parallel relationship or else prepared in the contemporary context, is responsible for a screen of prophecy that is indispensable to the aspirant in his legate discipline. At that time the whole schematism becomes truly esoteric. It creates a white magic for the cultivation and sustainment of a higher dimension or a prophetic potentiality of mind.

A third weekly lesson is provided for the aspirants who

at their option select astrology as an added area of investigation, and the materials of this category are sent out in an order suitable for each of them individually. There are weekly letters from the Chancellor to the regular students, that is, members of the Assembly of all classifications collectively, and they are known familiarly as the blue letters since thus far in the Sabian project they have been mimeographed on paper of that color. They too are in a cycle of approximately twenty years. Reports on current world affairs from a prophetic perspective, and currently known as the white letters, are issued every other week. They are for the legates primarily, but are shared with everyone. Special messages for the acolytes and the regular monitors, that is, those who do assigned work in consciousness for the Assembly, are sent out monthly and so far on yellow paper. There are special agencies for the exchange through the mail of current experience and information, such as the Chancellor's Fortnightly Field Notes distributed to all regular students. There are also the tape recordings of conferences or discussions available in circuit together with the typescripts made from them and supplied to subscribers.

The acolyte lessons are arranged for fortnightly attention over the five-year period. For the first acolyte year the *Arcane Sacraments* seek to lead the aspirant into the way by which he may orient himself to his own experience in the terms of his own highest potential. In a second year the orientation suggested to him through the *Racial Cycles* is in terms of the rhythms of human history, to the end that he may begin to establish his own immortal succession in a significance that will remain ever worth while to himself and his fellows. The *Divine Mantras* in his third year offer him a discipline in the corresponding spatial orientation, or point him to an enduring social competence through a control of meanings by a proper use of language and so give him a start in mastering the occult semantics. For the fourth year the *Sabian Tarot* presents a technique for the immediate evaluation of experience in any particular convergence of potentialities and consequences, that is, for the recognition of laya centers and the realization of what may be needed at any special moment for their development and maintenance. *Pythagorean Number* in a fifth year sustains an initial appreciation of the initiate's capacity to bring all relationships to pattern according to his own choosing rather than leaving this to capricious circumstances he is unable or unwilling to bring under conscious direction.

There are no special legate lessons. The aspirant of that grade is expected to bring major attention back again to the regular issues with at least some grasp of the screen of prophecy they establish, and so with some sense of the prophetic potentials of his own consciousness. If he wishes he may have, for supplementary weekly consideration, the twelve series that deal in order with the magic squares of idea or the *Sabian Absolutes, Occult Dichotomy, Magic Squares, Corner Patterns, Cabalistic Depth, Dimensional Reality, Patterns of Circumstance, Patterns of Function, Patterns of Activity, Patterns of Experience, Geometrical Symbolism* and *Dimensional Symbolism*. These expositions of pure cabalistic concepts have a special continuity, and so should be taken in regular sequence. They are issued in normal course to students of the astrology discipline, following the twelve sets dealing with the stellar art in its usual terms. It is presumed that by then the cabala, as here developed out of Ibn Gabirol, will reveal the larger implication of the horoscopic principles and hence in a way constitute a transcendental astrology quite independent of the planets and heavenly mechanisms.

It is most important that the Sabian method of study be understood by the neophyte from the very beginning. First of all he must remember that, through the whole of his immortal ongoing, any point of origin is within himself. Hence source for him can never be identified in a physical or even divine locus conceived as lying outside his own ultimate self-pointing. The Sabian lessons and materials to which he now has turned to instrument his inspiration will with but few exceptions come endlessly in cycle, and he starts his work with them as they happen to be in issue at the time of his affiliation with the group. There is nothing more unusual in this than in the fact that a baby is born into human history in its current course, but the apparent accident of particular moment for an aspirant's entry into Sabian consciousness will become increasingly significant as he persists on this particular path under the Solar Mysteries. What is required of him at the start is an attitude of mind, amounting to an open receptivity to every potential of his own experience. He is to accept no authority as established by anything other than the fact of his own dependence on it, that is, he is to render unto Caesar the things which are Caesar's. This means a respect for parents as long as he remains in the home of his childhood, and a full acceptance of the social rights of the community in which he finds it convenient or necessary to function. But in general and above all else he is to learn to become the sole author or sponsor of his own responsibility.

The initial step for him is to cultivate the flame of his own inspiration or creative comprehension. To that end he is asked never to try to remember the content of Sabian lessons or other materials for the reason it might seem to be a duty or a privilege to do so, but rather to enter into them quite at random and as far as possible at the stirring of a rapport deep enough within himself to suggest at least a measure of initiative seated in his own laya center. Under the discipline as a neophyte he should give some attention to the various books and papers at least once a week, whether these be the current issues or anything coming into his life then or previously as a direct or indirect result of his self-dedication through the Assembly, and this if possible should be at a regular time and under some consistency of circumstances. However, he must realize that to strain to meet the ritualistic ideal is to develop the very sort of crystallization he may be seeking to escape. Meanwhile, and in a simple way of putting the matter that has grown up in Sabian practice, he is asked to window-shop in the materials primarily or at least to pursue no point except as a particular interest is quickened. And then and by the same token he is to continue the pursuit only as this interest remains alive, or seems to justify the attention he is giving it. Indeed, if he is successful each week in finding a single challenging idea he has more than met the minimum requirement of his obligation. He may go as far as he likes, of course, and in whatever manner he chooses. But the activating impetus in all he does, in connection with his progress on the Solar path, must spring from the very real depths of himself.

The Nature of Sabian Authority

Since anything is to be said to be what it does, in the terms of an Aristotelian axiom employed continually in the Sabian project, any authority is to be seen as constituted out of the exercise of itself. It is in this sense that Jesus, in the New Testament account of his life, is reported as speaking with authority. In the exposition of the principles built on the Ibn Gabirol magic squares, and made fundamental in Sabian understanding, authority is identified most characteristically by the pleasure it gives to obedience. In complementation with the ultimate necessity that man must mind his own business and thus serve his fellows only as he is successful in making (1) their concerns his own and (2) his outreaching an expression of their potentials as well as his own, authority becomes a phenomenon of that multiformity of interweaving divisions of labor through which the conscious individual becomes a social or in essence a spiritual creature.

Authority under the Solar Mysteries always flows into channels and personalities where its exercise is a maximum convenience to those concerned. This is the essence of democracy, at least in theory. Through the whole of man's history the recognition of the elders as the council of final resort in all dispute has been a simple acceptance of the fact that an individual learns to epitomize fruits of the experience of his fellows in his own character, and so with maturity to reveal the developing wisdom through the universality of understanding he is able to share more and more with others. Equity or chancery law is the legal recognition of the two-way nature of right and privilege at root, and such a pioneer in the modern science of jurisprudence as John Austin found he had to stress the importance of enforceability in legislation if it was to be effective at all. The use of compulsion under a dictatorship is high dramatization of the ultimate weakness of a rule when a popular sanction for its edicts is lacking. In consequence the mode of approach to man's welfare through acts or decisions imposed on him for his own good is identified in the occult tradition as Lunar, and seen as of transitory value if not almost immediately destructive in its results.

In order that they may be framed properly in the Solar vision, all activities in connection with the Sabian project must be autonomous. They are given every liberty of modification and nonconformity to demonstrate that there is no authority imposed from above but rather only that which rises out of present and entirely individual participation in the Eternal Wisdom. Group leadership is by a convenience of initiative and endowment, or of all that follows in train as in teaching and administrative experience or prestige and skills that can be adapted effectively from other activities and opportunities. It does not remain fixed but continues as by an acclamation that is implicit if not explicit. Thus the continuance of the author as Chancellor rests on no more than the general recognition of his role, and of his effectiveness in its performance. As far as possible all details of operation in the group are worked out through the discussion of other or prior experiences with higher reality, to the end that the procedure thus given form may in turn become part of a continuing great tradition.

Authority of a secular or religious nature can be of very real value to the person achieving administrative or pedagogical responsibility under the Solar Mysteries, but it is by no means a necessity. Thus ordination by some established religious body or graduation from advanced study along scientific or intellectual lines in some commonly recognized institution, or both, certainly will facilitate the Sabian contribution of the seeker who has the temperament as well as the time and the means for this collateral accomplishment. Any desire for achievement of this sort is encouraged, and any actual effort is helped in all ways possible.

There is a species of symbolical ordination or hieratic succession in the arcane tradition, but while actual enough it is more a dramatization of the continuity of effort toward some transcendental goal for the welfare of the race than a description of any fact meaningful in itself. Some major historical service in the preservation of the esoteric insights as a living organism of realization may require that the given worker in each incarnation make a new contribution, as in the production of what it is convenient to identify as an occult master thesis. A heightened facility for accomplishing this may involve the re-creation of former and well-tested loyalties, or in a sense a preservation of a succession in a particular authority through a laying on of hands by an initiate server about to decease. In the usual case, as encountered or experienced by the average aspirant, the establishment of a chain of conscious continuities is a less exceptional and more ritualistic strengthening of the ageless heritage. There is a covert reference to this in connection with the fifth step of the opening evocation in the healing ceremony. Specific details of this sort of course are not any part or parcel of the Sabian project, unless they happen to provide a consideration proper to the legate level. It is merely important to realize that the chancellorship of the Sabian Assembly is not determined in any way by considerations restricted to a particular student. Under the Solar Mysteries the office cannot exist in the line of personal successorship characteristic of a Lunar dispensation.

The Study Group

The usual plan for a study group is a weekly meeting at a regular time and place. It may be closed or open to the public, and in the former case visitors should be permitted but with a definite rule covering the frequency or nature of visiting by prospective members. The sessions may be directed by one or more of the students in regular pattern, and any sort of rotation in various roles may be arranged by common agreement. Every effort should be made to encourage questions and to further discussion, to the end that each student in attendance has a maximum chance for actual sharing or creative participation in the rehearsal of whatever enduring insights may prove pertinent for the moment. In general all classwork should be based on Sabian materials, but of equal value to the invisible fellowship is the interchange of ideas when Sabian principles and methods are employed through other subject matter in the approach to a broader or deeper comprehension of the self and of the world in which it functions. There is no need to hold to a given topic during any particular session, or to attempt to round out any consideration unless the additional attention to it seems promising. None of those present should ever be permitted to monopolize the time, or to pursue any line of exposition that fails to quicken and hold the interest of the others, but by the same token each of them should have his right to his say in turn.

A Sabian class is opened normally with the *Intonation of the Sacred Vowels* and closed with the *Benediction of the Elements.* An alternative dismissal, appropriate when the emphasis at a given session has been more on the heart than the head side of realization, is the *Admonition to the Senses.* If in the use of the *Intonation of the Sacred Vowels* it is desired to provide a more obvious stress of the seven-and-five symbolism of major and minor vowels, distinguished by the four-line stanzas and two-line couplets, half the latter may be omitted according to taste. If the meeting is open to the public, and a collection is taken, the *Blessing of the Offering* should be employed in the manner suggested for the chapel service. If convenient, study groups should be held on Monday when the approach to the materials is mainly a matter of mind, and on Wednesday when it holds more to the devotional pattern. When the Sabian healing ritual is used at the beginning of the study group the usual invocation for the start of any classwork is omitted. And by the same token, if the healing ceremony is added at the end of a study period, there is no need for the customary class dismissal.

Some Details of Ritual

Any substitution or rearrangement of ritualistic detail

is the privilege of each local group, but the invisible fellowship is strengthened when the Sabian forms are employed for activities concerned primarily with materials and procedures of the Sabian vision. All its rituals were developed at the specific request of the sponsors constituting the invisible council, to the end that the project as far as possible might have a creative originality of its own making. In this fashion its experimental or laboratory nature is preserved, and its laya center is protected from unsuspected orientation to alien potentiality. On the other side of the coin, however, the Sabian Assembly invites a free and unlimited use of its ritualistic forms by all who may care to employ them. The flow of their inspiration and revivifying power is to be outward and in broad dedication to the occult tradition at large.

Music may be used as an integral part of any Sabian activity, either with actual performers or by means of recordings. The type employed should be determined by its general acceptability to those who are asked to listen, and its place in the program at any particular meeting should be left to individual initiative and group taste. Refreshments may be served at any point in any gathering of Sabian aspirants as well as in the acolyte study where they are required, and they may be of any nature suited to the taste and temperament of those participating. When there is such a breaking of bread it may be preceded by the *Grace to the Elements* of the private devotions.

Neither the use of subdued lights nor the burning of incense at Sabian meetings is encouraged in a modern generation that generally is oversensitized to psychological impressions, unless in some particular case the group of students happens to be thoroughly familiar with spiritualistic phenomena or drilled in proper safeguards for heightened self-integration under psychic conditions. Smoking should be permitted at classes and public sessions during lecture or discussion periods if those present are people among whom for the most part the use of tobacco is common, but not during any ritual or at healing and restricted sessions where the objection would be the same as to incense. Greater latitude within reason may be given at outdoor gatherings.

By contrast the burning of candles, as made a necessary or recommended part of some ceremonies, may be helpful at other classes and meetings whenever it can be done with aesthetic results and without affront to participants of marked anti-Catholic inclination. The lighting of them should be formal, immediately following the opening invocation, and all so lighted should be extinguished normally in the course of the closing dismissal. If food is served after a meeting they may be permitted to burn until the first of those who have broken bread is ready to leave, and extinguished then during a moment of silent appreciation of the fellowship.

Rituals may be read, but when possible they should be memorized and recited. During any of them those present when not standing should sit erect without knees crossed or fingers contracted. In outdoor ceremonies there is an advantage of bare feet on the ground, and bodily surface relatively free for contact with the air and sun, since such added and primitive rapport with nature facilitates the dimensional outspread of a civilized man handicapped to some extent by his cultural inhibitions. Care must be used to avoid procedures that might outrage the sensibilities of any given community, but in general and otherwise the aspirant serves his own spiritual progress through every physical or bodily satisfaction of a healthy sort. Sports and competitive exercise of muscular skills on the one hand, and the fullest possible participation in the creative arts on the other, can be a particularly valuable adjunct to self-fulfillment under the Solar Mysteries.

While the lily-and-snake symbol may be employed for imprint on Sabian materials, and adapted for decorative purposes, no strictly Sabian altar, sculpture, picture, painting, inscription or anything even remotely ecclesiastical in suggestiveness is to be permitted. Every effort is to be made to avoid diversion of attention from the Sabian group as essentially a project-in-action and not in or of itself intended to become a separate tradition within the general arcane framework. In its vision it is anything but an organized establishment for the promulgation of ideas codified for once and all. As a further help in discouraging crystallization the members of the Assembly should avoid the use of the word Sabian as a noun, that is and for example, the reference should be to a Sabian aspirant and never to a Sabian.

The Healing Regimen

Under the Solar Mysteries any sort of spiritual assistance in a case of difficulty must be requested by the person in need before it can be given. An exception is provided by children or incompetents for whom others are responsible, and thus are endowed with the right to make the appeal, and by instances of ties so close that concern for a loved one is in no true respect a coercion. In Sabian procedures the healing functions are given their focus through the written requests presented in the prescribed form of a healing slip. This may be any piece of paper or other material on which it is possible to write, and that will burn or disintegrate in water when the time comes to dispose of it. In size it should approximate an ordinary business or calling card. On it should be put the date, a statement of the need in as simple and unspecific a form or with as much detail as may be wished by the person submitting it, and his usual or accustomed signature. Ink should be used, and this should be of the type containing iron or what commonly is found in the blue-black sort available everywhere. The minute metal content is important as an effective substitute for the blood demanded in ancient and medieval times. The slips should not be addressed to any power or agency divine or human, either in fact or mind, but should be permitted to speak in uncompromising impersonality for the inner and necessarily impartial core of a personal and eternal ongoing. Each slip should deal with a single problem or deficiency, but as many may be written and presented as are necessary to cover every detail of the help asked.

Healing slips are to be placed near the bed every night, and with morning are to be destroyed by fire or water. If there is no adequate privacy for the open display of the slips during the night they may be placed where they will be protected from the casual eye. The student in the inner Sabian work will use his private shrine at all times, both for his own slips and those of others, and this special repository may be in the form of a small Christian or Buddhist altar if the seeker is Catholic in his tastes.

An additional healing slip should be written weekly and if possible brought or sent to a Sabian healing meeting, Alternatively it may be sent to the Chancellor, or to any Sabian worker who conducts the healing ritual privately in connection with his work in consciousness. When practical all slips put in the mail should be timed to reach their destination on Tuesday, and unless convenience dictates otherwise all healing meetings should be held on that day.

Anyone requesting healing, in addition to writing his daily and weekly slips, is asked to devote a moment to special meditation on his need at least once during each waking hour when the meditative effort will not interfere with everyday activity and responsibility. He will be able to facilitate the healing process very appreciably through this repetitive centering of his thoughts and aspiration at the laya center of the more genuine self-realization.

A Sabian aspirant on the healing list may have recourse in addition to a practitioner of mental or divine healing, and he may resort to any sort of physical or psychological therapy to which he may be drawn. Prayer according to religious belief, or the use of affirmations in supplement to the healing requests, is entirely proper. To ask for healing from many sources is no more objectionable than consulting several specialists in many various areas of life. However, it is apt to be altogether fatal to results to ask for help in even one channel of divine orientation that is not approached with full faith and deep respect.

Any person who wishes may employ the regimen of healing slips entirely by himself, and in this connection perform the healing ritual in his own behalf. By the same

token he may invite any others to participate in healing
effort for their benefit as well as his own by asking them for
the proper slips, and by inviting them to join him in the
ritual, entirely as he chooses.

At a Sabian healing meeting the slips should be placed
in a bowl or other receptacle suitable for the procedure
to be followed, or they may be laid out in a place where
their privacy is protected. They may be placed before a
Christian or Buddhist altar if no prejudices are quickened
on the part of participants in the service. All details in
connection with the slips should be completed before the
start of the ritual, and just before the dismissal they may
be burned ceremoniously. If not destroyed by fire during
the meeting they should be torn in fine pieces and soaked
to illegibility in water immediately afterwards.

Where healing meetings are held regularly it helps the
focus of therapeutic consciousness if a glass jar of unre-
fined petroleum is kept on the premises. Its contents
should remain undisturbed and unused for any objective
purpose, but it may be moved about in any way and as
often as convenient. When oil so employed is no longer
needed or desired in connection with the healing regimen
it should be burned or soaked into the ground.

Healing slips should never be read by anybody receiving them or participating in the ritual, and they should
never be sealed in a special envelope. Because of possible
confusion with them, as thus protected in their privacy,
no Sabian communication should ever be placed on very
small pieces of paper.

A person is said to be on the healing list when his request is sent to the Chancellor, or to any member of the

Assembly conducting one or another healing function for the group in connection with healing quadrangles. In such a case an initial statement of the need must be made, together with regular reports on progress or lack of progress, in addition to sending the healing slips. This information is needed for the quadrangle meditation, and it is supplied to the quadrangles in conjunction with a first name. If possible, however, it is given to workers who do not know the individual for whom the spiritual assistance is requested. The procedure is quite apart from bringing or sending healing slips to the healing meetings. When any aspirant acting as an individual does work in consciousness for others he may or may not require a statement of the need, entirely as he wishes.

A participation in the healing meeting without writing slips, but with an inward or unspoken affirmation of the need during the period of silence in the ritual, is not only acceptable but often is fully as effective. It is helpful to supplement the slips with this inner statement of desired ends during the meditative quiet of any Sabian gathering, or whenever it is convenient to spend a few moments of meditation in an edifice open for prayer or quiet communion with God.

The thank offerings of those who request spiritual healing are monetary when the services of an individual healer are asked, or when the appeal to the Sabian Assembly is in connection with specific personal problems. In the case of the Assembly these contributions are handled precisely as other gifts, whether received through a collection at some meeting or sent to the Chancellor or other proper person, and are applied to the furtherance of its general

vision. However, when an aspirant asks healing as a detail
of his discipline, as when he seeks amelioration of individual financial situation in order to be able to offer at
least the minimum costs to the project of carrying him on
the roll, the thank offering is psychological or an intangible of which money cannot possibly be a token.

The Healing Ritual

The healing ritual begins with the *Evocation on the
Steps*. When conducted by an individual privately his
repetition of the refrain after each evocative stanza should
be through a silent mouthing of the words as a way for
strengthening the presence of the invisible workers he
needs for his purposes.

Next in order is the *Prefatory Acknowledgment,* followed by a silence of approximately five minutes for the
inward affirmation of healing needs. During the silence
a sole celebrant of the ritual may hold his hands with
palms downward a little above the healing slips, if he has
chosen to lay them out rather than placing them in a container, and he may remain seated if he wishes.

The *Consummatory Acknowledgment* closes the healing silence, followed in turn by the *Consecration to the Indwelling Spirit* and *Meditation on the Healing Gifts,* and
then finally by the *Healing Dismissal*. A sole celebrant may
find it suitable to use the *Prayer of Parting Adoration,*
prepared for private devotions, rather than the normal
closing.

During Holy Week each year the Sabian healing ritual
is directed to the quickening of the global consciousness,
and attention to individual matters of other than great
emergency is suspended completely. Aspirants able to

develop stronger therapeutic consciousness in an Eastern orientation may take the time of the Wesak festival for their annual sabbatical week in connection with their personal healing effort. This usually is at the full moon in May when the Theravada or Southern Buddhists commemorate Gautama's birth, enlightenment and passing. In general, however, the seeker should anchor both his initiatory effort and his spiritual service to his fellows in the laya center of the culture of which he finds himself a part.

The Steps in Solar Rehearsal

The Biblical book of Matthew in its relationship to the other New Testament materials has a general place of pre-eminence very similar to that of Isaiah in the Hebrew scriptures, and the fact is reflected in the primary importance given this Gospel in the Sabian analyses of Christian insights. Thus the studies in Matthew's account of the life and teachings of Jesus constituted the first Bible lessons in the project, and their issue began less than three months before the inauguration of the Sabian pledges or the formal introduction of a Solar initiation in the framework of the group activity.

The special place of Matthew in the history of the Christian church has been due in largest measure to its completeness, both in a literary and a theological sense. The organization of the contents is a superb example of creative craftsmanship, and as a whole it is remarkable for the extent to which it not only rounds out exposition with definite and practical explanation but also emphasizes the details of spiritual instruction most needed by the seeking soul of any age and culture. Indeed, the book has been a source of unending awe to scholars from the days of the church fathers down through the rise of higher criticism and on into contemporary times with their increasingly unbiased approach to all sacred writings. The Sermon on the Mount as found in Matthew is virtually the magna charta of discipleship under a Solar dispensation that has been inaugurated in the name of the Christ, or dramatized in the mission of the Nazarene, and within the present generation it has been possible to see the direct outflowing of the inner power of this unmatched compendium of spiritual insights in the satyagraha or soul force developed and employed by Mahatma Gandhi under its particular inspiration.

Matthew is the cabalistic gospel, and the consequent use of numerical schemes by its unknown compiler has been noticed by the nonoccult commentator from the earliest days of Christianity. The general pattern of the materials can be described most simply as an alternation of sections of narrative with interlarded discourses. Using a twelvefold division there are on the one side the accounts of (1) the beginnings, (3) the great works in dramatization of the ministry, (5) the failure of the people to catch its import, (7) the enlargement of the vision to what then becomes the real creation of Christianity, (9) the journey to Jerusalem, (11) the final events with the crucifixion and (12) the resurrection, and on the other side (2) the Sermon on the Mount, (4) the discussion of discipleship, (6) the interpretation of the Kingdom of Heaven to the masses, (8) the pastoral instructions to the disciples and (10) the eschatological passages or analysis of the end of the age for the disciples' benefit. If number two of these sections of the text, or the immortal sermon, is the handbook of Christian discipleship, then number seven is the heart of Solar initiation as it is epitomized in the series of steps that Jesus took in his definite revelation of messianic stature. The ordeals these steps represent are made quite explicit and so can be seen to be in close parallel with the spiritual experience of the average aspirant of the present day.

Initiation in an occult or spiritual sense can be defined most simply as an expansion of consciousness. The meditative and healing procedures as consciousness-expanding agencies are most effectively a rehearsal of the higher experience essential to any genuine illumination, and in consequence the heightened experience of Jesus in advancing his mission at the crucial point of the particular incarnation can be made an effective basis for the opening and in many respects the most important part of the Sabian therapeutic ceremony. The evocation is of an external realization that in very true fashion is beyond the individual aspirant except as he continues to rehearse its potentials in advance, over and over again with every quickening insight of what might be involved for him when he actually achieves a conscious immortality. He must learn that he never stands in any one fixed place, as on one step or another, but always is making his way onward and upward. The expanded comprehension takes form behind him quite literally, for his sustainment, and the broadening anticipations reveal their formless promise ahead of him as encouragment in his unceasing effort to consummate them.

The refrain of the *Evocation on the Steps* is a summary

of the whole of Matthew in its cabalistic depths. First there is this new law that will bind men as tightly as the old dispensation from Sinai, but with a binding that is of the inner aspiration and that is realized through a tireless outreaching for the wonders of the invisible fellowship. Then there is the spiritual rebirth or the inescapable molding of character through an unceasing quest for perfection, and this uncompromising self-regeneration in ultimate actuality becomes the immortal continuance. So much for the dedication within, or the way of the heart.

Then there is the mind, or the way of reason. And truly there are no threats to the seeking spirit half as serious as the twisted or half-formed ideas that seduce man in his very soul, and thereupon hold him not to the highest potentials he believes he is envisioning but instead to the self-sufficiency through which all ultimate growth is checked aborning. Hence Jesus in these chapters warns against the aimless persuasions of the word-quibblers on the one side, and on the other the shallow utopian notions of the professional busybodies all set to remake the world in the image of their own vanity. And finally there is the danger in the impatience of the mental or reasoning capacity that may betray man in the most shameless fashion of all. As superficially the conditioned creature, his growing inclination will be to cease effort in the face of the exacting requirements of any vision worthy of real pursuit, and to embrace instead the lesser values and easier rewards that cater to his weakness and give him his joy in witless dissipations.

The keynote of Matthew is in the Hebrew name Immanuel applied to Jesus from Isaiah, or God-is-with-us in

English. The refrain at the opening of the Sabian healing
service sings this most precious of all realizations, or the
fact of the presence. The song is of the true laya center
of self as eternally established and strengthened. The
seeker, for the actuality of his anchorage in all-being at
core, may well indeed demand that on the literal side he
be (1) bound to the immortal insight through his outreaching and (2) recreated in its image ever and ever
more effectively through his search, and on the imaginative
side that he be (3) held above all frivolous or empty concepts and (4) protected against even a most transient fall-
ing away from the highest activating vision.

The first step in Solar rehearsal was dramatized by Jesus
when he fed the five thousand or more people who had
followed him on foot out into the badlands. The incident
is recorded in Matthew, 14:13-21. The never-ending controversy over what miraculous elements may be involved
is of no importance in any larger significance of the event.
This was the point in spiritual history when the older
conception of a prophetic oversight of specially chosen
vessels, or of those who would live the eternal promise and
thereby demonstrate it to the masses, was subordinated
finally and irrevocably to the idea that the individual of
and by himself could now be brought into a personal relationship with God. Man at last is to be treated as an adult,
since the race can be said to have passed through its childhood. The dispensation of manna is succeeded by the
dispensation of the Host. The process, however, must have
its conscious recapitulation in the life of every seeker
quickened to his opportunities and thereupon readied for
his conscious immortality.

Here by the cabalistic correspondences of the arcane tradition is the Eucharist or sacrament of the token. In an alternative charting of Solar unfoldment (cf. *Occult Philosophy,* pp. 296 ff) the ceremonial giving of thanks enables the morsel to serve as the meal, and builds the consciousness of the full supply as this in its turn has every outer and literal manifestation in testimony to the laya center established and strengthened at the depths of the new selfhood. In the occult allocation of the sense specializations in the body the necessary first refinement of an eternal ongoing is through the eyes, or man's priceless gift of creative or spiritual visualization.

The second step in Solar rehearsal was dramatized by Jesus when he walked on the water in the night and in that manner rejoined the disciples he had sent ahead of him by boat. The incident is recorded in Matthew, 14: 22-33. Again the miraculous implications are beside the real point. It may be presumed that the multitudes responded to their experience of strangely gratifying satiety with an effort to preserve it in the literalized stagnations they were accustomed to confuse with reality. Thus they might well think to make the man of Galilee an earthly king, along the lines of their Messianic expectations and with little realization that they would only bind themselves anew to the older dispensation of a Moses and of manna. It is this obtuseness of the masses that demonstrates how little they may be touched to higher realization collectively or without an example life into which an individual aspiration could be brought to some initial focus. A mystical self-discovery encouraged by the saviour or the myth figure is needed to break the thralldom of bondage to an unquickened flesh, and in consequence it might be expected that these events of the still hours would be astral or of an invisible fellowship that often may be touched at the threshold of the dream state. Peter was quick to realize that this was something in which he should participate, but he was unable to frame it in anything but accustomed orientations and so he came to grief.

Here by the cabalistic correspondences of the arcane tradition is the sacrament of matrimony, or of the invisible fellowship. Nonoccultly it is a certification of the integrity of flesh as the life-sustaining and self-reproducing functioning of the organism, or a dramatization of its power of continuing in its own genius in terms of all the lower or higher vehicles of a conscious personality, and in the esoteric tradition it solemnizes the alchemical marriage or the stabilization of the transcendental capacities. In the occult allocation of the sense specializations of the body the necessary second refinement of an eternal ongoing is through the smell that is ever able to detect the real subtleties of existence, and that not only has long been a synonym for shrewdness and sagacity but that was employed in the Old Testament to describe the high sensitiveness of the godhead itself.

The third step in Solar rehearsal was dramatized by Jesus when he confounded the traditionalists who sought to trip him up on the matter of obedience to spiritual law. The incident is recorded in Matthew, 15:1-20. In the cycle of Solar realization it had been demonstrated that the approach to men's hearts through a satisfaction of their appetites is fundamentally an attempt to purchase their allegiance and hence a proof of the ineffectiveness of an overliteralized social gospel. By the same token the display of inner wonders to those unable to assimilate them into a genuinely personal reality had been seen to do no more than unseat all inherent self-confidence and so prove the futility of the ill-advised miraclemongering characterizing so many of the holiness groups in age after age. Now the Galilean had faced the question whether a departure from the rigid boundaries of the sacerdotal law in which these people had long rested secure would not be as profitless a procedure. Yet he must have realized that men and women after all have to make their own decisions, and stand on their own feet as spiritual adults, if the great line of prophecy is to have fulfillment in any larger dimension. The call at the moment had been to examine the inner stirrings and the wholly personal insights from which any true illumination would have to spring. Obedience might need a new reference, but that still would have to be self-centered at the end.

Here by the cabalistic correspondences of the arcane tradition is the healing sacrament of unction, or the restructuring of all reality at the core of itself and thus its ultimate orientation through the continual re-establishment of its own eternal rhythm. The anointing of the self in the dedication of its potentials and its aspirations is no more than the thoroughness of rehearsal, or breadth of ritualistic symbolism, needed for any transcendental sustainment of an ever-broadening experience. In the occult allocation of the sense specializations of the body the necessary third refinement of an eternal ongoing is through the taste, and this is less a simple recognition of flavor or the like and more a discrimination in the ap-

proach to life on any or all levels. Articulate speech provides the principal measure of a man, once he begins to
share his ultimate resources with his kind. The fellowship
then is above the level of mutual appetites, or of licking
tongues of either literal or figurative nature. The individual begins to become himself as the speaking and so
thinking or reasoning animal, and to reveal what self-
adequacy he may have developed.

The fourth step in Solar rehearsal was dramatized by
Jesus when he retired to gentile territory to think through
the problems met at the three preceding steps, and there
encountered the woman who challenged him to a broader
perspective as she sought healing for her daughter. The
incident is recorded in Matthew, 15:21-28. If the law
through which the Hebrew people had been sustained
through long centuries was no longer to be held in the
form of its effectiveness, through a reasonably literal adherence to its provisions, what then could be used to frame
the broadening insights that the Nazarene would bring for
a larger dimension of realization? Is anything ever fulfilled by breaking it down? It had become evident that
if the goal was to be sought through an attempted purification of society at large, or by an effort to quicken an
individual's inner and highly occult powers before he was
ready for illumination, the average man was hardly placed
on his own feet in terms of any spiritual adultship. After
all was there any answer in the concept of a new law, and
an educational program to establish it? Necessarily projected more or less in the pattern of the old, would it not
in time slip back into the old? As the prophet from
Galilee reflected on these things the Syrian woman made

her appeal, and responded wittily to his reminder that his mission was to his own people and that an outlander could hardly speak for the higher potentials that in her case had sprung from another if similar culture. Then it was that he gained the vital insight. An increase of transcendental dimensions must be marked by an equivalent increase on practical levels. His message must have a setting in a universality that would have real meaning to all people everywhere.

Here by the cabalistic correspondences of the arcane tradition is the sacrament of confirmation, or of initiation itself at root. The progress in understanding of each aspirant must have its own continuing seal of approval from those with whom he rehearses it. For the building to the goal it is ever vital that he enlist the participation of all who are able to grasp the meaning of his effort at each successive stage of quickening, and the old must always become the new by an experienced transition. In the occult allocation of the sense specializations of the body the necessary fourth refinement of an eternal ongoing is through the ears, or the particular concentration of attention at the core of any genuine self-continuity. The seeker believes as he hears inwardly. And through the music of the spheres he achieves an ultimate ordering in the rhythms of the Eternal Wisdom.

The fifth step in Solar rehearsal was dramatized by Jesus when he fed some four thousand seekers who were with him in the hills and had been without food for three days. The incident is recorded in Matthew, 15:29-39. Most Biblical scholars hold to the theory that one original occasion led to the three versions of a miraculous feeding

— taking John, 6:1-14, as a third — but in the cabalistic
Matthew the role of the repeated account is important
as representing the necessary psychological echo or con-
forming to the age-old doctrine that all deeper teachings
must be presented twice. The variations in the numbers
of people, loaves, fishes and baskets is of detailed esoteric
significance and shows the second event to be of the more
generalized order. The supplying of the need is more
definitely in orientation to the inner man, instead of his
outer appetites.

Here by the cabalistic correspondences of the arcane tradition is the sacrament of ordination rather than Eucharist.
It is the dedication of the individual to the task of exalting the understanding or realization of others, and of giving thanks for them in ceremonial fashion as he makes himself the myth figure or the incarnation of their hopes and
expectations in one fashion or another. After passing the
focal point in this rehearsal under the Solar Mysteries the
aspirant must turn from the concern over himself as the
individual with a private potentiality, and begin to see
himself the eternal Servant precisely as the Nazarene has
done before him. He learns that it is with the hands that
man blesses as well as serves. In the occult allocation of
the sense specializations of the body the necessary fifth
refinement of an eternal ongoing is through touch or the
actual and creative immediateness of a true spiritual ministry. The worker in the great vision assimilates himself
continually to his fellows, and in doing so establishes himself in some one or another division of spiritual labor
under the Solar Mysteries.

The sixth step in Solar rehearsal was dramatized by

Jesus when he confounded the legalists a second time and then rebuked his disciples for failing to distinguish between the superficial reality of everyday life and the true bread of the spirit. The parallel is with the rebuke for lack of faith when Peter attempted to walk on the water, and the incident is recorded in Matthew, 16:1-12. The orthodox critics of the Galilean's ministry made their attack in the first instance on the ground that the disciples did not pay proper attention to the ceremonial ablutions, and now or in the spiritual echo they had sought to trap him with their guileless request for a sign from heaven. After exhibiting their shallowness again in the context of their own choosing, he proceeded to give them the sign of Jonah. The naïve and unquestionably fictional prophet who had no liking for his assignment to Ninevah had discovered the simple truth that he and God could never get very far away from each other, and that he moreover could never be himself very adequately except as he was God-manifest-within-himself. In other words he had to become in his own person the idealized Emmanuel that the man of Nazareth was born to be, and that all men indeed may become once they are willing to enter fully into the Christian salvation. The leaven of the Pharisees and Sadducees to be avoided was the infectious rationalization that refers all responsibility in experience to exterior and alien factors.

Here by the cabalistic correspondences of the arcane tradition is the sacrament of baptism rather than unction, and so the turn from healing as merely the reordering of things-as-they-are to the complete rebirth from new source and new realization. Selfhood is quickened and requick-

ened into its immortal potentiality here and now. As
seeking souls baptize and are baptized continually in their
invisible fellowship, or in a transcendence of time and
space, they create the frame of Eternal Wisdom in which
the new hope of the race has more than adequate foundation. In the occult allocation of the sense specializations
of the body the necessary sixth refinement of an eternal
ongoing is through the mind, or what Aristotle identified
as the common sense and what ultimately is the fullness
of an individual's intuitive powers. The aspirant through
reflection or his continual rehearsing of his insights is able
to understand and so consummate his own true destiny in
a dimension far larger than mere selfhood.

The seventh step in Solar rehearsal was dramatized by
Jesus when in response to the mysterious identification
given him by Peter he declared the key to illumination to
be the immortal binding which is made the basis of the
refrain for the *Evocation on the Steps*. The spiritual echo
is of the primary emphasis placed on what comes out of a
man's mouth rather than what is put in it, and the incident
is recorded in Matthew, 16:13-20. What comes to a head
here is profoundly esoteric. Superficially Peter merely repeated what from the narratives would seem to be a common acceptance. It is obvious that more is implied than the
acknowledgment of the messiahship when the Nazarene
turned to his irrepressible disciple and addressed him as
the son of Jonah. Occultists often make the interchange
a mutual recognition of prior incarnations, or of Jesus
revealed as David somewhat obliquely through the form
of address and Peter revealed as the bumbling prophet
sent to the Assyrian capital. The discussion as a whole

would certainly seem to be in terms of reincarnation, and there is no reason to suppose the doctrine of personality rebirth was unfamiliar to any even half-literate Palestinian. However, the reference more probably was to Jonah as a sign, and to Peter's realization that what the Nazarene might be said to be after all was what he was busy in being. The question that was being asked around, as to who he was, would then be added to the foolishness already characterized as the leaven of the contemporary emptiness of thinking. The affirmation can then be seen to be to the effect that the chance for initiation or personal immortality was being brought to all.

Here by the cabalistic correspondences of the arcane tradition is the sacrament of penance, or the full of self-responsibility brought back in ageless repetition to the laya center of selfhood or to the continual restructuring of each individual's personal ministry to his fellows. In separation from God the seeker is lost to his destiny, and for his enduring fellowship with those of like mind with himself he must return to the first step and in the eternal Eucharist make a new start on the way. In the occult allocation of the sense specializations of the body the necessary seventh refinement of an eternal ongoing is through man's reason, or what in modern days might be identified more specifically as his universalizing capacity. In the Biblical psychology it is the thinking said to be seated in the heart. His inclination to be this and that, or thus and so, is the true determinant of his being. Let this ego or will of his be exalted, and he is incarnate in every vision of the race. Thereupon he becomes a custodian of healing power for every individual hope of his fellows.

In actual experience of course the steps are taken more or less concurrently, and with every variety of succession or overlapping in view of the temperamental needs of each aspirant. The ordering through the life of an avatar, or in the schematism of a Bible or a textbook, is necessary for understanding and reflection only. The approach may be made with possible advantage from more than one point of view. Thus *Occult Philosophy* makes use of the somewhat different strand of the occult tradition, in dealing with the sacraments, but in no respects offers either contradiction or negation of insights.

The Chapel Service

Devotional services in connection with Sabian activities are usually conducted by established religious groups in some one or another phase of co-operation with Sabian objectives. The chapel service is for an occasion when group devotions of purely Sabian alignment are desired. Normally it begins with the healing ritual for a first fifteen minutes, with or without use of healing slips as circumstances dictate. The *Healing Dismissal* is omitted and instead the *Sabian Doxology* is sung, if musical accompaniment or adequate song leadership is available. Otherwise it is recited, or it can be omitted. Next in order is a devotional address or an inspirational program. If a collection is taken the *Blessing of the Offering* is pronounced with those present asked to hold their gifts in their hands during the blessing. The Sabian affirmations for the current two-week period are then recited in unison. The services are closed with the *Sabian Benediction*.

An effective way to use the affirmations is to repeat each one three times in unison with a different emphasis for each repetition. Thus, if the affirmation is "I rely on the healing power of God within me," it may be first, "I rely on the *healing power* of God within me," then, "I rely on the healing power *of God* within me," and finally, "I rely on the healing power of God *within me*." When varying emphases are employed the places of stress will have to be announced just before the repetition of each affirmation, or some other indication provided in advance for those participating in the ritual. Or the leader may make the statement each time as he desires to emphasize it, with all then repeating it together.

The Ceremonies of Dedication

The Sabian chapel service is used when there is occasion for a *Ceremony of Dedication*. This then takes the place of the address or inspirational program, in whole or in part. When there is a talk in connection with these ceremonies it should be in the nature of a testimony or eulogy on the one hand, or of exhortation and encouragement on the other, and its position in the order of service should be immediately before the dedicatory ritual itself. The celebrant, questioner and all individual respondents should be selected in advance by any process the given group finds convenient or pleasing. In general all present remain seated except when directed to rise in the course of the ritual, but those who speak should stand while making response or asking questions. All four ceremonies begin with the same opening statements and related queries, but each continues according to the proper part for the particular dedication.

In the rare case where it seems imperative to have more than one type of dedication at the same gathering the dismissal at the end of one is omitted and the celebrant continues with the altered question, "And to what additional spiritual task are we asked now to bring our consciousness?" Every effort should be made to avoid this contingency.

If at all possible and convenient the dedication of a life should be at the bank of a stream of running water, or in easy view of one. When this is not practical the symbolism may be preserved by appointing someone to bring pure water forward, or to pour it from one container into another, as reference is made to water as the most liquid of the elements. If desired the celebrant may use some of the water from the stream or any significant source to make a gesture of baptism during the moment when all in unison affirm the dedication out of the eternal ocean of potentiality.

If at all possible and convenient the dedication of a departure should be (1) at the side of the grave, (2) in the presence of the ashes of the deceased or (3) at some place where he has labored and expended himself. The celebrant should have a bowl or small container of earth for use in symbolizing the inert matter into which the physical substance of the departed one is to be committed. He should let this pass through his fingers while all present are making their acknowledgments in unison of the integrity of nature. While the dedication is made he may dust a little of the earth on his forehead, and thus symbolize the creative memory sealed eternally in the invisible fellowship through which the dead and the living are still to be linked.

If at all possible and convenient the dedication of a

partnership should take place in surroundings of particularly sentimental association for the participants, or under circumstances of unusual spiritual significance for those who take part in the ceremony. A fire in an outdoor setting or an open grate, or a mass of candles otherwise, should be provided as a background for the ritual. As acknowledgments are made to the radiant energy of the cosmic fire the celebrant or someone appointed for the purpose should light candles left unlit to this point. As the dedication is given in unison, out of the endless fructification of all reality, the celebrant should light and present a special taper to each of those dedicated in this fashion. Each of them in turn, as he makes his individual affirmation, should blow out and then relight the taper of his partner or partners. Thereupon both or all shall hold their lights until they are told to resume their seats at the end of the dedication, at which time they shall extinguish them as best they can in a single and simultaneous breath. In this ceremony the partners shall decide in advance in what order they shall speak in accepting the dedication.

If at all possible and convenient the dedication of a project should be under circumstances that dramatize the significance of the particular vision in some exceptional fashion. If it is a house or other building or any sort of premises for which dedication is asked, the place for the ceremony is indicated of necessity. This also is the case if it is a shrine or religious edifice of any nature, a place for regular meetings, a center for such specific activities as a library or school, a dormitory or workshop of any kind, or the quarters for any type of business or manufacturing enterprise or for any sort of social service or community activity. The pattern is much the same in dedicating a series of meetings or conferences, or even a single gathering of unusual importance. For an intangible entity such as an association or a corporation, or an excursion or a mission, the representation is either through officers or individuals particularly involved or by papers of authority as a legal charter and the like. The eternal breath is best represented objectively by a dance or music, and those present may be requested to stand during the dramatization of its presence. Meditation and any form of religious devotions will serve if shaped for the given occasion to a point of sufficiently dramatic impact. During the statement of dedication in unison the celebrant should raise his hands in benediction, and seek to direct the inflowing blessing to give it a symbolical effectiveness.

The order in which participants speak up in rededication at the ceremonies should be arranged by the celebrant beforehand. It may be very helpful if other subordinate details are worked out in advance, in accordance with good taste and the inspiration of the moment, and indeed and at all times the goal in the performance of the Sabian rituals is the greatest possible degree of encouragement for individual creativity and the consequent manifestation of an eternal sustainment.

The *Dismissal at Dedication* may serve as the formal closing for the whole service when the taking of an offering and the recitation of the affirmations are omitted.

The Full Moon Meeting

The Full Moon Meeting was the first of the Sabian ritualistic ceremonies to take a definite pattern, apart from the earlier use of the liturgical forms for opening and closing the class sessions, and as such it has been the core of the ordered initiatory procedures under Sabian auspices. It is fundamentally the rehearsal of a seeker's progress upward to each facet of his illumination, and his consequent return downward for service to his fellows. It has been and remains of prime importance in any quickening and requickening of individual morale at the laya center of conscious selfhood.

The time for the assembly normally is the last half hour from 10:15 to 10:45 p.m., as shown by the common agreement of the local clocks, that can run its course before the precise moment the moon is full at the place of meeting. A tabulation of the days and dates of these special half-hour periods for each United States time zone is supplied the students once a year, and the continuity of the celebrations by the Chancellor from the beginning is shown by the number of the session. Also shown is the corresponding lesson to be taken from the *Message of the Hierarch,* and this determines the proper *Statements of Realization and Thanks* to be selected. It is the option of any particular Sabian group to establish a continuity of its own, and thus to designate its sessions from their beginning and to use the 1st lesson at that time and so on as long as the chain of observances remains unbroken. It is permissible to begin in this independent fashion, and to start all over again whenever desired, at any convenient lunar month. In special emergencies the meeting may be held according to the time of some adjacent or even distant time zone, provided only this does not place the meeting in a different calendar day.

The ceremony may be conducted by two, three, five or seven aspirants, without reference to the additional number who may be in actual attendance. When seven are used, different questioners interrogate the legate, acolyte and neophyte spokesmen in turn. When five, the questioner is the same person throughout. When three, the legate, acolyte and neophyte parts are combined. When two, the celebrant adds the questioning to his normal role.

Members of the Assembly unable to attend a regular ceremony may go through the ritual by themselves at the proper time. This enables them to share in the general consciousness and so gain its upliftment, but the performance under these circumstances does not create the situation necessary for attendance in fulfillment of the acolyte obligation. Any name signed at this time can only be for the symbolical contribution to the individual sensitiveness. When the ritual is used in this manner the celebrant and questioner parts should be spoken aloud and the legate, acolyte and neophyte statements made voicelessly or by whisper.

Candles should be used if at all possible, and they should be lighted immediately before or during the *Invocation to the Living Flame.* The privilege of lighting should be rotated through those participating in the ritual more or less regularly in person. At the close of the ceremony, or immediately after the *Chaldean Dismissal* and before anybody has had a chance to move, the celebrant should extinguish the candles.

Attendance at the Full Moon ceremony is restricted to (1) regular Sabian students, (2) members of their families and their house guests, (3) representatives of the civil authorities or well-established religious or educational bodies desiring to investigate Sabian activities and (4) people present at a prior Sabian meeting in the same quarters on the same evening. In the last instance the formal closing of the preceding meeting is omitted. An opportunity should be given for those who have been in attendance to leave if they wish, and some explanation of the ritual should be given to those who choose to remain. By house guest is meant any individual who has broken bread with a Sabian aspirant in the aspirant's home during the calendar day in which the ceremony is performed.

The signing of the names should be at a table where each aspirant may sit in turn as he does so, and always in a signature book used specially for this purpose. As far as possible those present should stand in a semicircle for this part of the ritual, and the order of signing should be counterclockwise through the arc. In all other circumstances the celebrant should arrange the order of signing in advance. Each one signing should come forward in his proper turn, and then go back to his place. Not until then should the next in order make any move. All present should sign, including any nonmembers of the Assembly. The celebrant should repeat each name aloud as it is written in the book, and add an audible thank-you. Those who bear proxies made out to them should sign the additional names after their own, repeating each aloud as they do so and then delivering the proxy forms to the celebrant. He should continue to add his thank-you after each proxy signature. If there are proxies made out to him he may designate some aspirant to come forward to sign first and to remain standing at his side until all others

have come forward. Thereupon the celebrant should take
his place at the table to sign the names of those designating him as proxy, either as he reads the names aloud himself on signing or as they are read aloud for him by the
aspirant he has designated to do so. He should repeat
each name aloud as he signs, and in all cases add his
audible thank-you. When every name has been signed he
should write his own in the book as witness and thus as
himself present.

The proxies and signature books shall be sent to the
Chancellor or the esoteric secretary appointed by him
whenever they are requested for examination, or they may
be handled in whatever other convenient way is prescribed
from time to time. Proxy forms should be simple, to the
effect that the aspirant appoints a given person as his
proxy to sign him in as present at a Full Moon meeting
of a given date. They must be dated, and signed in ink.
In emergency a proxy form may be telegraphed but no
person may be designated a proxy by telephone. After
the ceremony the proxies should be filed as any other
correspondence, and thus kept available for reference in
the case of any confusion.

At the close of the meeting each aspirant, as far as possible in decent conformity to the social amenities or in
meeting any of the necessities of physical existence, should
go home and to bed without conversation or special activity such as might dissipate the consciousness gained at
the core of self.

The astrological symbolism of the ceremony requires no
consideration of appreciably technical sort. The annual
passage of the sun through the zodiac has been taken from

ancient times as an allegory both of man's spiritual progress in general and of any individual initiation in particular. The successive ordeals in the earth life of an
avatar, as charted through the zodiacal signs, are known
collectively as the solar myth and taken to dramatize an
inevitable recapitulation of the history of the race in the
lives of each of its great initiate leaders. The very considerable uniformity of events in the careers of the mes-
siahs from age to age becomes a pattern for the spiritual
outreaching of the seeker, and thus can provide an essential underlay of significance in the ritual. Astrology in
even its everyday horoscopy reflects the great myth through
its doctrine of the heavenly man, or the schematism pic-
tured in the oldtime drugstore almanac with the signs
of the zodiac distributed to the organic parts or divisions
of labor in the human body. This anatomical correlation
gives a language for the ceremonial rehearsal of the Solar
ordeals.

The cycle of Aries-Cancer is the symbolical head-to-
stomach arc in the cosmic organism, or the succession of
(1) aspiration or the desire to be alive, (2) expenditure
and replenishment, (3) taking and outgiving of the psychological vitality and (4) the personal rehearsal of existence. Here lies the conscious control of all experience
as the work of initiation on the legate level. It is the
recognition of fullness in the realm of self, and a concomitant repudiation of everything in life from which no
welcoming response can be gained or with which no creative reciprocity can be quickened.

The cycle of Leo-Scorpio is the symbolical heart-to-
genitals arc in the cosmic organism, or the succesive neces-

sities for (1) the poise of simple aliveneess or a basic
health of body, (2) the poise of social co-operation or a
fundamental gift for the assimilation of reality to self in
an everyday prosperity, (3) the poise of a more definitely
personal or self-distilled relationship with others as made
manifest in a resourcefulness of temperament or a root
happiness and (4) the poise of a genuinely rational administration of self and its powers or the continual creation and refinement of a foundation understanding. Here
lies the conscious control of personality as the work of
initiation on the acolyte level. The occult discipline
strengthens a cleansing of consciousness at the laya center
of responsible selfhood, and a consequent elimination of
all useless accretions in the outer being. Spiritual healing
is facilitated by a consistent and rigorous repudiation of
any or every element of experience from which all
possible potentiality of sharable worth has been extracted.

The cycle of Sagittarius-Pisces in the symbolical thighs-
to-feet arc in the cosmic organism, or the successive emphases of (1) incarnate flesh as the basis of the personal
fellowship through which all higher realization must be
sustained, (2) the bony structure in the body as the basis
for any moral stability in either individual or social aggre-
gate, (3) the blood circulation or the flow of consciousness
as the basic instrumentation of all group fellowship or
practical social integrity and (4) the lymphatic or self-
policing capacity of the human organism as the basic organization of all conscious effort to achieve a perfection
of the self and its world and thereby pave the way for
aspiration at the threshold of any next dimension of seeking. The correlation of thighs to flesh, of knees to bone,

of ankles to blood and of the feet to the lymphatics represents astrological technicalities that hardly would be obvious to the layman. Through these curious correspondences, however, lies the continual enhancement of experience in its essentially naïve potentiality as the work of initiation on the neophyte level. The arcane discipline furthers an elimination from the aspirant's everyday realization of all the stultifying inhibitions and senseless prejudices that have been allowed to clutter his thoughts and to confuse his instinctive reactions, and strengthens a concomitant and increasing rejection of every potentiality of experience from which nothing of enduring worth will ever be gained.

In the first of the three periods of silence the aspirant should attempt an inventory of his spiritual progress on the path, and to observe through his inward examination where he may have failed to meet the fullest challenge of the responsibilities he has accepted on achieving his present level in the discipline. In the second period of silence the inward self-inventory should be directed to his co-operation with the healing ministry of the invisible fellowship, and with the work of the great Lodge in helping sustain the steady rhythm through which the race itself has an underlying and continual rehearsal of its experience. In the third period of silence he should seek to recommit himself to the fullness of his aspiration through any meditative means that may help him envision it, and thus re-enthrone it as an enduring reality in his own ongoing.

The thanks to which the aspirant gives expression, after his statements of realization for the current lunar month, are addressed to the living flame of divine aspiration as this must be quickened in the spiritual depths of every true seeker of the Solar path.

The Message of the Hierarch

The Old Testament book of Isaiah has always had a marked pre-eminence among Hebrews and Christians alike, and with the discovery of the Dead Sea manuscripts in 1947 it has been curious to note that the monastic community at Qumran apparently held the Isaiah scrolls in particular veneration. The new evidence direct from two millenniums ago suggests that the text was much more settled in form than that of any other of the prophetic collections, and the fact that this section of the Biblical writings came to be so central in the development of the Sabian project is rather striking indication of the integrity and self-rectifying power of the arcane tradition as it comes to a modern fruition in the Assembly.

Isaiah like nearly all Old Testament books is of composite authorship. The prophetic contribution of the man who gave his name to the whole, and who carried on his ministry in Jerusalem through the latter half of the eighth century B.C., not only is restricted to chapters 1-39 but in all probability comprises a relatively small part of that first of the main sections of the book. Biblical scholarship did not come to recognize and demonstrate the multiple nature of the compilation until the eighteenth century A.D., and it was more than a century later before chapters 56-66 came to be identified by many authorities as a third work perhaps as largely complete in itself as the two preceding. Neither conventional nor occult knowledge of the Bible has reached any degree of ready and adequate answers for the innumerable questions arising from the text in the form of its present survival. It is possible however, and with real certainty, to chart the great scenes of prophecy with which the whole sixty-six chapters are concerned. First was the era of Assyrian supremacy and the narrow escape of the Southern Kingdom in the days of the original Isaiah. The second offers a change of scene to Babylon at the time of the forty golden years of Nebuchadnezzar. This was the period 604-561 B.C. and four-odd decades exceptionally important in the esoteric tradition. The third locale is back in Jerusalem when Ezra and Nehemiah were faced with the many problems consequent on the return of a considerable number of the exiles about the beginning of the fourth century B.C. It is with the Deutero-Isaiah of chapters 40-55 and the sixth century B.C. that the Sabian project is most vitally concerned.

In 1892 the hypothesis of the Servant Songs was advanced, and a vast literature has developed around the controversy and the almost insuperable problems involved. Ultimately as many as ten of these songs have been recognized by various scholars, but a consensus of opinion that squares rather interestingly with occult knowledge of the matter identifies a total of four, namely, 42:1-4, 49:1-6, 50:4-9 and 52:13-53:12. Parenthetically it should be remembered that the Biblical divisions of chapter and verse do not always make particularly good sense. They are arbitrary and relatively recent, with not too much agreement on the facts of their establishment. The modern chapter divisions may be the work of Lanfranc in the eleventh century or of Stephen Langton at the beginning of the thirteenth. The Old Testament verse divisions are probably the contribution of Rabbi Nathan in the fifteenth century, and apparently the New Testament verses were given their present form by Robert Stephens in 1551. Any occult significance of the numbers of chapter and verse in consequence is apt to be rather fortuitous.

Bible scholars who accept the Servant Songs as actually of separate composition from Deutero-Isaiah proper consider them interpolations or a later insertion, and this theory raises many difficulties through the quality and aptness of the verses as mere additions. The arcane tradition sees the connection more happily through reversing the order of relationship. Marie Corelli has fictionized the original drama of the insight in her *Ardath*, but any verification of the events by normal historical methods is impossible. It need only be reported that according to occult knowledge the songs were the work of an unknown poet and reputedly precocious youth who inspired a more mature and equally unknown but highly dedicated scholar to the writing of Deutero-Isaiah, and to the consequent preservation of the poetic gems by embedding them in the wonderful vision of Israel's messianic hopes.

Out of the limitation of Babylonian prosperity and the materialistic version of the good life, seen as in reality the worst of all captivities of the soul, came what has proved to be one of the greatest voices of all time to speak up for the truer destiny of man and to reveal the essential nature of an avatar. The anonymous writer and a sort of real-life prototype of Corelli's Alwyn, leaning on the parallel and unexampled insights of an almost contemporary Jeremiah, lifted up the promise of the new covenant conceived by the man of Anathoth and proceeded to set

the stage for Jesus and for a fresh and outer ramification
of the Eternal Wisdom in the Western World. His work
is hailed by James Muilenburg in the most recent and
ambitious of Biblical commentaries, the *Interpreter's
Bible,* as the noblest literary monument bequeathed from
Semite antiquity and as such to be ranked not only with
Job for epic stature but with the writings of Paul and
Augustine for perceptiveness and imaginative insight.

It is significant in the unfoldment of the Sabian vision
that Richard G. Moulton's new edition of the *Modern
Reader's Bible,* published in 1907 at the very moment
when the author of this manual was making the contact
with source materials and languages of which he gives
account in the foreword of his *George Sylvester Morris,*
should place dramatic emphasis on Deutero-Isaiah. The
identification of these sixteen chapters as the Rhapsody
of Zion Redeemed made an indelible impression on at least
one creative mind reaching out slowly to grasp and use
its powers. It was thirteen years later, or on December 26,
1920, when David James Burrell, at one time interested in
Theosophy and a brilliant expounder of the Scriptures at
the Marble Collegiate Church on Fifth Avenue in New
York City, preached a sermon on Deutero-Isaiah's 44th
chapter and in so doing and without knowledge of the
fact provided sudden added breadth and depth of inreaching and its tie back to Babylon and the Sumerian culture.
The author then was thirty-two, preparing to begin his
work as executive secretary for a world's convention of
young people and thereby about to precipitate events leading in turn to the first mobilization of Sabian group potentiality. That took place in the Judson Tower at the

foot of the same Fifth Avenue, an even two years afterwards.

The adaptation of the 44th chapter for occult purposes
came in California in another two years, when the author
was asked to prepare material of an esoteric sort for the
inner students at the headquarters of one of the established
occult societies. It was then that the mode of adaptation,
soon to key the formation of the Sabian rituals, was in-
vented in the course of a long solitary session in the most
available equivalent of the Judson tower. In still another
two years the sudden need for a strictly Sabian Full Moon
ceremony was met by the initial employment, for liturgical
purposes, of this highly arcane interpretation of man and
his propensity to idol worship. From that evening forward
it has been an integral part of the substance or the life of
what for long was the one Sabian observance of consistently ceremonial nature. The fuller exposition and
explanation follow now after thirty years of unbroken
continuity in its use.

The term recension is given an expanded and in a sense
an inversion of meaning in Sabian usage. Thus what is
implied is not any literal recovery of a better or truer
meaning, or any degree of return to an initial expression
of concepts that have been twisted from their first import,
but rather a development of the ideas in their suggestiveness or enduring allusion in order that an original stimula-
tion or power of insight may be recreated for use by a
later and different culture and psychological set of mind.
The technique has been perfected to facilitate a measure
of standing on the shoulders of giants. What is to be seen
literally is a paraphrase of a given text, with no effort at

verbal translation but instead a free interpretation or what might be seen as a cradling of new realization in the convenient form of the old.

The composition of the so-called Rhapsody of Zion Redeemed has been recognized almost universally as the work of a single inspired mind, although suffering some emendations and a little editing, and it can be broken up into identifiable segments such as then can be seen fitted into the more or less haphazard mosaic required by the spirit of oriental poetry. Chapter 44 presents an introductory five verses at the beginning and a summarizing four more at the end, and in substance and respectively these framing conceptions are part of a preceding presentation of redemption by grace starting in the 43d chapter and of a vision of the anointing of Cyrus that runs into the 45th. Out of this rather exceptional fortuitousness of chapter division the recension gains its outer or fourfold frame of two parts starting and two parts closing every individual's lunar cycle of experience. In the structure of the poem as thus delimited, and as the Bible scholars almost invariably outline it, there is a section concerning Yahweh's glorification of himself in Israel consisting of verses 6-8 and 21-3, and this provides the occultist with a convenient inner and also fourfold frame or two parts adjacent both to the beginning and the ending. The recension does not follow the scheme quite literally, however, since verse 5 is paraphrased for the inner rather than the outer frame. Then there is the core of the chapter, in the satire on the idol maker that rightly is regarded as among the finest examples of irony in all literature, and this provides a dramatization for the five ordeals.

What the *Message of the Hierarch* presents, as in contrast with the steps of initiatory focus dramatized on the
basis of Matthew's text for the purpose of rehearsal in the
healing ceremony, is the cyclic ebb and flow in the realization by the self of its own being as at core a ceaseless
spiritual experience. It is not the ritual of an accomplishment, but rather of the process of conscious continuousness as this takes place round and round the cycle of the
lunar year. There is no possible beginning or ending,
and the designations of the lessons as 1st and on through
13th is for convenience in identifying the sequence and
no more. In the strictest of occult terms there is here a
measure or a charting of the psychic acuity of the seeker,
or of his rushing forward and pulling back in sensitiveness
on his approach either to a reality higher than anything
he yet has known or to a potentiality greater than his own.

The first lesson is the *Assurance* (verses 1-2) or the regrasping of the cycle after the *Eternal Promise* and the *Fulfillment* preceding it have re-established the outer frame
with a somewhat impersonal application. The orientation
is to be made personal through the second lesson, and in
the *Outpouring* (verses 3-4) the aspirant is encouraged to
spill out the wholeness that he will be seeking again after
a season in which he has opportunity to mature a little
more and so reorder his own distinctive ongoing.

The third lesson is the *Dedication* (verses 5-6) or the
move towards self-establishment in the change of self-
orientation from the outer to the inner frame, and in the
adoption of a special form of act and reaction to identify
the aspirant's seeking among his kind. The fourth lesson
is the *Witnessing* (verses 7-8) or the fulfillment of the

responsibility the seeker has assumed. Here is the certification of his self-assignment in this more intimate of the spiritual frames of reference through which he proposes to function.

Thereupon come the five ordeals that as a group alternate in the arbitrary annual cycle of subjective or spiritual experience with the group of eight self-orientations and their consequent acceptance by reality in general. The fifth lesson or first ordeal is the *Great Shame* (verses 9-11) or the experience of humility as the self periodically and of necessity must discover how far it can fall short of its own expectations of itself. The sixth lesson or second ordeal is the *Adoration of Self* (verse 12) or the experience of emptiness as the aspirant in due course must discover that a mere exercise of his potentials in their potentiality is hardly the outgiving by which alone the being is able to know its fullness. The seventh lesson or third ordeal is the *Surrender to the World* (verse 13) or the experience of frustration when the reality of the self is measured by whatever of universal and eternal promise may be brought to its manifestation. The eighth lesson or fourth ordeal is the *Great Futility* (verses 14-17) or the experience of self-debasement as the things of God are seen through their ridiculous counterfeit in man's audacious pretence to eternal worth. The ninth lesson or fifth ordeal is the *Bitter Lesson* (verses 18-20) or the experience of disillusionment as the self, with some recapture of its better sense, is able to see itself more clearly and to shudder at the inevitable self-judgment it must face.

The tenth lesson or the *Exhortation* (verses 21-2) is the desperate outreach again to the security of the inner or intimate frame of self in the general reality of the world, and the ultimate regaining of a basic spiritual aplomb as the inner ear is opened and the seeker experiences the call of self to its true service for its kind. The eleventh lesson or the *Indwelling* (verse 23) is the purification of self as through the catharsis of its ordeals it finds itself for the moment again at peace in the core of its being, and thereupon is fit to receive the divine incarnation in some one or another phase of eternal realization.

The twelfth lesson or the *Fulfillment* (verses 24-5) is the achievement of the new power and potential. The thirteenth lesson or the *Eternal Promise* (verses 26-8) prepares the aspirant once more for his pilgrimage. As he comes to grasp the spiral nature of all genuine evolution of the spirit he is able to bring more and more of himself to the ever-repeating phases of realizations ahead, but as conversely he fails to keep the light strong and bright before him he falls into the more and more meaningless revolution of the cosmic wheel and so does not even know that for him there is no longer any creative distribution of his destiny.

The Quarterly Meeting

The quarterly meetings that have broad correspondence with the summer and winter solstices are sometimes also designated as semiannual meetings, and in normal course they are gatherings at which the public at large is particularly welcome. One is held on the evening of July 3d and when possible in conjunction with a summer conference of Sabian or like-minded aspirants. The other is a watch-night service on December 31st. The two quarterly meetings that have equally general correspondence with the spring and autumn equinoxes are held on Palm Sunday and October 17th. The latter date is used because it is the formal birthday of the Sabian Assembly. The emphasis at these is placed on the fellowship in discipline of the Sabian students primarily, but there should be no restriction of visitors.

Quarterly meetings should be opened with the *Challenge of the Hierarch*. This has a special spiritual power as the first liturgical form prepared in anticipation of Sabian use. It is a recension of the 82d Psalm, which according to the record in the 10th chapter of John's Gospel was cited by Jesus in his important interpretation of man's nature and of the creative relationship between prophet and God. It remains the basic and eternal challenge to the aspirant under the Solar Mysteries.

At the sessions of solstitial correspondence on July 3d and December 31st the first order of business after the opening is the recognition of the neophytes who have made affiliation with the Sabian Assembly in the preceding six months, or who are present at one of the semiannual gatherings for the first time since signing the neophyte pledge. They should be brought forward or asked to stand at their places, but if there are no new students present some other aspirant should be selected to come forward or stand to represent the newcomer in general for purposes of the ritual. The *Welcoming Address* is given, and then time is allowed for other pertinent recognitions such as accomplishments in the Sabian project of immediate or local interest. Next is an inspirational program in the form of an exposition of some section of the *Message of Ezekiel* by a legate or perhaps an aspirant of lesser grade who has been chosen in advance to prepare his talk. The *Discourse on Inspiration* is presented, and then there should be opportunity for any member of the Assembly present to give testimony to what he has learned of the significance of the Sabian work to the world and to himself, and what in consequence he has been able to develop for himself and share with the world. A general discussion of Sabian activities and their potentiality may be interesting and profitable. The meeting is closed with the *Prayer to the Fullness of the Year.*

The program is similar for the sessions of equinoctial correspondence on Palm Sunday and October 17th. The recognitions, however, are for the students entering the acolyte work at the particular time. No ritualistic identification of these aspirants by person or by name is permitted, as anything of the sort might contribute to an appearance of spiritual distinction among persons. Rather someone shall be selected to represent the new acolytes symbolically and collectively, and to come forward or stand as the *Discourse on Achievement* is presented. On Palm Sunday a general inspirational address or program should be arranged, with its subject an evaluation of the preceding twelve months of events on the world stage and an interpretation of whatever spiritual trends may have been revealed. On October 17th the inspirational activities should center around a consideration of achievements in the Sabian project during the preceding year, and this should conclude with a spiritual interpretation of the Solar Mysteries vision as it has had particular manifestation in current Sabian effort. If possible this latter feature should be a group presentation worked out in advance by a special quadrangle of acolytes and legates. The inspirational part of the program on Palm Sunday and October 17th should conclude with a ritualistic and impersonal recognition of those entering the legate discipline, on exactly the same pattern as the acolyte recognitions earlier in the meeting. The *Discourse on Stewardship* is given, and then testimony and discussion follow as at all quarterly meetings. Closing again is with the *Prayer to the Fullness of the Year.*

The Message of Ezekiel

The prophet Ezekiel, as one of the giants of spiritual insight, is as great in importance as he is elusive when it comes to any dependable knowledge about him. His book in the Old Testament canon is in about the worst textual condition of any, and it has been the subject of controversy from the earliest times. Indeed, there are few questions about it that can be answered with any certainty. The throne-chariot vision, the ingestion of wisdom in the form of a scroll and the various repetitive details of the commissioning constitute a first three chapters that probably are of a single authorship and that are the basis of the Sabian recension. Out of all the mystery involved comes the power of this inspired material, and it is of exceptional value as a catalyst for the developing realizations of candidates on the Solar path of initiation.

With the epitomized *Master Thesis of Ezekiel,* one of the most brilliant of conceptions in all the arcane tradition, the mind may catch itself up in the broad creative sweep of the cosmos itself. In the astrological symbolization is given an expression of the illimitable meshing of all things in common cycles and mutual consummations.

The *Calling of Ezekiel* that frames the master thesis is the cabalistic self-ordering compacted into this small compass and revealing the achievement of fitness as an expanded perspective made manifest through a self-conscious adequacy of being. The key realization is that whatever is fit must act in the full of the fitness, if it is to continue adequate and creatively aware of itself and of its place in a general context of significance. Thus the candidate takes cognizance of what, in his way of thinking about it, must be a commission and a challenge.

The *Commission of Ezekiel* is the realization difficult above all realizations. Whatever is true to itself is arrogant to that which would challenge it from without, but yet is ever and infinitely receptive to that which comes from within as an expression of the inner self. In consequence the commission under the Solar Mysteries must be self-bestowed, not so much from the inward awareness of the self that springs to expression prematurely and so is arrogant and only stirs up ugliness from others but from the inwardness that listens first to the voice within and so learns to speak to an inwardness of others that lies behind their own superficial arrogance.

The *Ordination of Ezekiel* is gained by every seeker who is caught up in the wonders of the cosmic order to which Ezekiel gives testimony in the master thesis and who thereupon adds a new testimonial of his own out of his different and necessarily unique and personal experience. The external form of this testimonial of the aspirant may be another master thesis of sorts, or whatever else might serve to dramatize the ability of a worker under the Lodge to enter the inwardness of others and so call to them with the true effectiveness of the Solar initiate. The aspirant is fit in the ultimate sense when his perspective is universal, or embraces every last facet of individual difference in those about him.

The *Ministry of Ezekiel* exhibits the gift for speaking with authority. This is the supreme mark of a genuine illumination, and ultimately it must be gained by every aspirant under the Solar Mysteries. It is the individual's mode of expression expanded so that it speaks to each other man and woman only as he has somehow become the total of all of them within himself, and thereafter is able to voice whatever may be the best of each of them in turn.

The Acolyte Meeting

The acolyte sessions are closed to all but acolytes and legates, but as at Full Moon meetings an exception is made for members of the family, house guests and representatives of well-established institutions or any civil authority desiring to investigate Sabian activities and practices. At the beginning the door should be closed temporarily for the *Meditation on the Solar Breath,* and then opened to admit tardy members. Candles should be lighted after the door is closed again, according to any simple ritual the group chooses for itself, and extinguished immediately after the *Acolyte Dismissal* in similar fitting fashion. The discussion should center at all times on the acolyte lessons. Sessions preferably should be fortnightly. A breaking of bread together should be a regular feature, and this should be before the candles are extinguished unless it is necessary to move to another room.

The leader of the meeting first presents the *Meditation*

on the Solar Breath in its entirety, or without a break. He
then announces, "The meditation on the cosmos, or on all
manifestation as a whole," and (1) repeats the first two
lines of the first stanza, (2) again repeats the two lines,
(3) repeats the third line twice, (4) repeats the fourth and
fifth lines, (5) again repeats these two lines, (6) repeats
the last line twice. Without any break he announces, "The
meditation on the vital principle of being," and proceeds
in the same fashion with the second stanza. Similarly he
announces, "The meditation on the emotional principle
of being," and proceeds in the same fashion with the third
stanza. Finally he announces, "The meditation on the
intellective or encompassing principle of being," and
proceeds in the same fashion with the fourth stanza. He
closes the meditation by repeating the last line of each
stanza in order, and emphasizes the closing by employing
a different tone of voice. In the meditative consciousness
the first three lines of each stanza articulate a spiritual
outbreathing, and the last three a complementary in-
breathing.

The Sabian Pledges

There are three sections in the Sabian neophyte pledge.
The initial section is the preamble, and consists of paragraphs *A* to *D* as a rehearsal of principles essential to all
self-committal under the Solar Mysteries. The first of
the principles is the necessity of (a) a supreme desire for
illumination, (b) a determination to become the Servant
envisioned in Deutero-Isaiah and (c) a realization that the
way is a conscious self-ordering within the Eternal Wisdom. The second of these principles is the necessity that
any conscious functioning in a reality beyond time and

space be sustained by a self-assumed obligation that can symbolize it in the everyday existence to which all lesser aspiration is limited. The third of these principles is the necessity that the cabalistic correspondence of the aspirant's higher self-realization with the normal consciousness of the spiritual group be recognized, and that the immortal consciousness of the individual be furthered by framing his self-assumed obligation in the identity of purpose characteristic of the group. The fourth of these principles is the necessity that the desire for illumination be established as an actual laya center for the aspirant's immortality through the dedication of all efforts of the self to ends in which the vision of the individual and of the group have a common manifestation.

The second section or paragraph 1 of the Sabian neophyte pledge is the actual committal, and it consists of the statement of the self-assumed obligation made in such fashion that it (a) may shape itself gradually as the personal but yet ineffable prior or true laya center for the conscious immortality, (b) never may be other than the effort to be what it is and thus never may be subject to the risk of any judgment of its success or failure in being what it is, and (c) as that which is eternal and universal in every respect of itself may be beyond every possibility of necessary relationship with people, organizations, communities, allegiances, loyalties or anything that can be reduced to definition or identification in a world of physical reality.

The third section or paragraph 2 of the Sabian neophyte pledge is the earnest, or the matter of the superficial tokens through which the initiatory process is rehearsed through the two solar years. In the arcane tradition all the deeper teachings are given twice for the fructifying and gestating emphases respectively by which they are established in the consciousness of the race, and the aspirant has the symbolical two cycles for achieving a measure of awareness in his immortal laya center. The two phases of the earnest are (a) the rhythmic ingathering to self of the Eve or the life as the whole-potentiality epitomized in the Eternal Wisdom and (b) the equally rhythmic outgiving or sharing of self through the contribution up from the substance of the Adam or ground of personal potential. This is an earnest because it is as the aspirant remains steadfast in his desire, thus given an initiatory instrumentation, that his Sabian pledge or obligation can be seen to have become his own in any actuality. Otherwise it has no import, and the fact need be no embarrassment to him and in no way an occasion for disappointment or a stumbling block to good feeling.

The written reports of those who do not attend study groups may be made (1) to the Chancellor directly or his designee, (2) to some member of the Assembly sponsoring the particular neophyte in any formal or informal fashion or (3) to any member of the Assembly willing to supervise the newcomer's adjustment to Sabian materials and procedures. In all cases the supervisory role shall be undertaken only at the neophyte's request or with his approval, and should be subject to change whenever he wishes. Except where the seeker and his correspondent for this phase of his discipline agree on some other plan, the weekly reports should be aggregated and submitted monthly. Only aspirants of legate grade should undertake any supervision of the neophyte's correspondence in fulfillment of his pledge. In cases of absence, when students are participating more or less regularly in a study group, the written report should be sent weekly to the leader of the given group.

There are three similar sections in the Sabian acolyte pledge. The initial four paragraphs *A* to *D* are again the preamble or rehearsal of the principles essential to the establishment of the seeker's tangible obligation on the level of the Servant or in a dimension next above everyday existence in time and space. Here is the proposition of group endeavor rather than individual discipline as the focus of aspiration under the Solar Mysteries. The principles are the necessity for (1) a recognition of a personal expansion of consciousness that can be identified as a measure of stewardship in the manifestation of the Eternal Wisdom, (2) a further recognition that the commissions of this stewardship are ultimately of the two or three working together in the name of the Eternal One or only-begotten principle of being, and not the result of any individual seeking as such, (3) a realization that the consistency and worthiness of everyday action and attitude that has contributed to the expansion of consciousness must now be given a larger dimension through undertaking new duties in connection with the invisible fellowship and (4) a determination to match the spread into space created by group effort with the needed and concomitant self-projection in time resulting from an enlistment of past experience in both present and prior lives, and the accompanying proffer of all future potentialities for service under the Solar Mysteries.

The second section or paragraph 1 of the Sabian acolyte pledge is the actual obligation, and it is a repetition of the neophyte self-dedication with now the (a) inclusion of the whole span of incarnations and (b) exclusion of dependence of any sort on even the intelligences functioning on other planes of reality. The third section or paragraph 2 of the Sabian acolyte pledge is the earnest, or the token obligations to the Sabian Assembly in (a) the continued sharing of personal capacities and means and (b) the ritualistic rehearsals through the work in consciousness in general and the Full Moon ceremonies in particular.

The annual reports required of acolytes are made to the Chancellor directly, or his designee in the given case, and all correspondence in connection with acolyte or legate discipline is confidential and similarly is with the Chancellor personally or the special designee.

There are three sections of like pattern in the Sabian legate pledge. The preamble in paragraphs *A* to *D* rehearses the principles essential to the establishment of the aspirant as a worker for the Solar Lodge on the level of the avatar, and the proposition here is the immortal contribution to ultimate ends of the race as not only a matter of group endeavor but also of an actual or collective continuance in organic form of some total body of dedicated souls through a span of history or in an establishment of an unbroken continuity in some phase of the esoteric tradition. For the average aspirant the avataric goal is achieved in what to him may seem an exceedingly insignificant foreshadowing of a Gautama or a Jesus, but it is no less an important contribution to the total vision and in the meanwhile it is essential for the everyday dramatizations that might hope to further the leavening of the world at large. The necessities are (1) a recognition of an earned place of identifiable nature in the racial destiny, (2) a further recognition that this has not been gained except through the personal associations that bridge mere physical incarnation, (3) a realization that the consistencies of action and attitude that have contributed to the enduring and spiritual self-recognition must now gain a very practical authority in the outer and practical world as an insurance against megalomaniacal pretension or self-destructive delusion and (4) a determination to sacrifice all dependence on self-identity by a transfer of conscious existence into a genuine racial embodiment of some experienceable sort.

The second section or paragraph 1 of the Sabian legate pledge is the actual obligation, and it is the dedication to the avataric role of the Servant in some definite particular and the strengthening of this with a surrender of all reliance on an anthropomorphic God or any reality known in any fashion as alien or external to the purity of laya center. The third section or paragraph 2 of the Sabian legate pledge is the earnest, or the continued token obligation to the Sabian Assembly in (a) the sharing of personal capacities and means and (b) the ritualistic rehearsal through the work in consciousness on legate quadrangles and its esoteric reinforcement at the four seasons.

Summary

The Sabian procedures are arranged at all points to provide a private or a group rehearsal of spiritual experiences and insights, to the end that these may become increasingly a part of the aspirant's very being.

The Sabian lessons are designed to provide the greatest possible spread over all areas of experience in order to further a breadth of such rehearsal, and the method of study places the primary emphasis on the stirrings of interest within the aspirant's own consciousness in order to launch him on the way of Solar initiation. He is drilled continually in the fact that his illumination springs from resources lying at the core of his own being. There are weekly issues of lessons on the Bible on the one hand, and on philosophy and symbolism alternately on the other, and in these two series there is neither beginning nor end but rather a continuous rotation of the materials through an approximate twenty-year cycle in each case.

The study of astrology is optional. There are special lessons for the acolyte's orientation to (1) his own instinctive ritualization of his values, (2) the cycles of history, (3) the hidden powers of language, (4) the unrevealed potentialities of anything of immediate concern and (5) the cabalistic patterns behind all reality. There is additional instruction with which Sabian students are supplied in various special cases. Discipline letters and other materials are distributed to the members of the Assembly in regular course.

Authority under the Solar Mysteries flows into channels and personalities where its exercise is a maximum service to all concerned. Sabian procedure demands that individuals and groups mind their own business in every possible respect. Classes and other functions possess complete autonomy. As far as is practical the project maintains no headquarters and avoids unnecessarily centralized administration. It is very careful to avoid constituting itself a church, or a fraternal order or any form of organization in which there could be a hierarchy of superiors. There is a hieratic succession in the arcane tradition, but this has nothing to do with the chancellorship of the Assembly or the leadership in any enterprise seeking to instrument some phase of the vision.

There are recommended programs for all Sabian activities, with ritualistic forms to use in the various connections, and all details of procedure are made available for those inside or outside the Assembly who might find them valuable. The study class is arranged to encourage a full range of discussion in connection with the Sabian materials and to further a genuine rehearsal of spiritual experience.

The healing ministry is of fundamental importance in the Sabian project, and its efforts are centered in the healing meeting and the work in consciousness. Written healing slips are employed in this connection, but while they are encouraged they are not made obligatory. There is a chapel service to meet any demand for purely Sabian devotions.

There are rituals for the dedication of (1) a life, in some parallel with the baptism of the church, (2) a departure, in a measure of correspondence with the graveside rites of the church and fraternal orders, (3) a partnership, with some resemblance to a marriage ceremony but embracing business partners and any other possible relationship of personal intimacy, and (4) a project as special premises or enterprises.

The Full Moon Meeting each lunar month is the heart of the initiatory rituals in Sabian work, and is of special concern for the acolytes. The quarterly meetings on Palm Sunday or Easter eve, July 3rd, October 17th and December 31st are vital to the inner discipline and are of special concern to the legates. The acolyte meeting is classwork with a special ritual.

Important and central events in the life of Jesus, as particularly dramatized in the highly cabalistic Gospel of Matthew, are used to chart the steps of Solar initiation for the ritualistic purposes of the healing meeting. The section of Isaiah stemming from the Babylonian captivity is of high occult significance, and a paraphrase of the 44th chapter is employed to give a ritualistic depth to the Full Moon meeting. At that meeting the cycle of the lunar year is used to rehearse the ebb and flow in the seeker's transcendent or psychic sensitiveness, and the ceremonial charting of his progress through the zodiac permits the concomitant rehearsal of his struggle to fulfill himself through his own individual manifestation of the Solar Myth. The opening chapters of Ezekiel, including the prophet's master thesis, are used in similar paraphrase for the quarterly meetings in July and December as a catalyst in the legate approach to the Eternal Wisdom.

The neophyte, acolyte and legate pledges consist of three sections. The preamble presents the four basic principles operating on the level of obligation in each case. The actual obligation is a committal to progressively greater degrees of spiritual or immortal self-reliance, and the earnest is the token self-dedication in the three outer dimensions of Sabian discipline at the portal to the Solar Mysteries.

THE SABIAN PHILOSOPHY

Philosophy is of great value to some aspirants, and little more than meaningless jargon to others, depending entirely on temperament and background. It is a useful tool of mind, but by no means a necessity of illumination.

The term was coined by Socrates, and its original meaning was love of wisdom. Now philosophy is the established systemization of the knowing process, or of thought and thinking, and on the practical side it is the analysis of the abstract or generalized realizations on which theology, science and all moral and aesthetic conception depend. In any ultimate sense it is the ordering of the mind's inreach to an understanding of man and its outreach to a parallel understanding of the world or the total complex of existence of which man finds himself a part.

Sabian philosophy classifies as a dynamic idealism, since it considers reality the actualization of a potential and never an existent in itself. It classifies also as an experientialism, since the real is accepted as that of which anything in question is ultimately the source rather than the product.

The Primary Statement

The world is ideal, but its ideality is expressed by its continuous maintenance of itself and not by an intellectual derivation of its existence from an idea or from any agent or source fundamentally or originally exterior to itself. At no point is it the end result of a process or of any mechanism. Rather it is organic and both (1) material, as encountered by the senses or measured by the tools of science, and (2) rational, as ordered by law or principle when approached through the mind.

Man also is ideal, with his ideality revealed in his moral nature or inner life, and he no less is both a material and rational being in his everyday manifestation of a physiological and a psychological identity.

The world and man are directly complementary to each other, and experience is the actuality of the interaction involved. Experience is (1) inclusive, since it represents nothing other than itself, and (2) competent, since it is always a conjoining of cause and effect.

Anything whether tangible or intangible is known through its characteristic behavior, or as it presents itself in experience.

The distinction between sensory and rational experience, or man's two modes of realization, is a functional division of labor and not the representation of an actual dichotomy in nature. Reality may be approached on the side either of the senses or of the reason, or on what the esoteric tradition knows as the heart or the head path of experience, as convenience may dictate.

The First Axiom

Knowledge already possessed, whether right or wrong, is the sole basis of further knowledge. This is the axiom of necessary prejudice, or of the inbuilt presuppositions on the basis of which behavior and judgment may become automatic.

Philosophy is the history of philosophy, that is, primarily an examination of the ideas by which men have ordered their lives in the past and a consequent determination of what may be expected when they seek to order them by the same or similar ideas in the present. Thus philosophy becomes a study of the mind's assumptions, or an analysis of what an individual may take for granted and thereby either facilitate or impede his progress toward the goals he sets for himself.

Since the mind of necessity is analyzing the content of its thinking with the thought habits and patterns of which it is constituted, that is, within a matrix of its assumptions collectively, it tends to rationalize everything into its own accustomed grooves and thus to defeat any attempt to break through its bondage to its own limiting ideas. The difficulty has been identified as the psychologist's fallacy, or assuming that thinking can be free of personal presuppositions. These are essential, and they must be left unquestioned if thought is to be possible. Consequently a disciplined intelligence must learn to make proper corrections in every conclusion to which it comes. To gain any impartiality the mind must function through the ordering of the thoughts or thinking capacities of minds of greater scope than itself. This ultimately becomes a participation in the community of mind on which modern science depends and of which the Eternal Wisdom consists.

Here is Newton's realization that the giants of understanding in human history are those who stand on the shoulders of giant intelligence before them. Thus philosophy of necessity builds on tradition. The philosopher, however, must be careful not to lose himself in an obsession with the past or with a supposed infinite wisdom of changeless aspect from the beginning, and destroy his competence because he forgets then that knowledge is valid only in its continual verification through experience. He must realize that he always stands at the center he creates for himself in the vast complex of man's ideas, and in this realization he becomes and remains a focus of thought for his fellows. As the thinking animal he is fundamentally a social creature, and he achieves for himself because he is achieving for more than himself. It is because of this that he can break through the ring of his lesser prejudices, and in doing so replace them with the greater ones that release rather than limit his efforts.

The process of breaking through limitation is known in the arcane tradition as initiation, or more simply as an expansion of consciousness, and the Sabian philosophy dramatizes the necessities involved by requiring the seeker to (1) know what he knows, (2) know what he doesn't know and (3) know what he doesn't know he doesn't know. This means that he begins to refine his knowledge by learning to define his terms or his knowing and thus be able to make accurate statement in any account of his outer experience and inner reactions. While doing this consciously and consistently, as he chooses to push his realization in any given direction, he discovers what more or less inevitably must follow in any given sequence of events. This is the way of knowledge through analogy and probability that actually leads to a knowing of the not-known. With this refinement of his reason he finds himself more and more in fellowship with the mind potential beyond his own, and in time he has access to the knowledge of which otherwise he would be totally unaware.

In such fashion he achieves a stage of seership, and he begins to find himself across the portal of the Solar Mysteries.

Here is the Sabian conception of a pure philosophy. It is free, and consistently creative, and though in many respects it may seem beyond all immediate usefulness it yet forever opens limitless new areas of a potential experience.

By its canons all things must be brought to their center of reference at each given point of contemplation or issue. In direct experience the center of reference is self. When there is a manipulation in experience of factors other than the self the centering is in the idea representing them in the thought processes of the self or of other selves similarly, and any idea so used is considered at work and is identified as a concept. The Sabian philosophy is termed the philosophy of concepts, since its principal function is to organize ideas for intelligent employment, and the concepts that have the most important roles in the Sabian project are given the form of keywords.

The Sabian student is expected to recognize the integrity of his own experience, and in time to order each and every detail of it in terms of the concept patterns through which he approaches the Solar Mysteries.

The Second Axiom

Everything that purports to be true is true. This is the axiom of necessary faith.

If philosophy is man's experience with ideas, religion in parallel fashion is his experience with truth. Religion is man's rehearsal of those elements in experience through which he has created an expectation beyond his own unaided hopes and powers.

In this enlarged fulfillment of himself he has come to know God, and in his inspired outreach beyond familiar limitations he also has come to know himself as a personage. He has acquired a dignity greater than mere animal training and rational conventionality. In his expanded consciousness he is the initiate, if but for the moment of his devotions. As he uses the powers he has unlocked within himself, and as he employs the higher potentials he has created for himself, he is able to serve his fellows. He becomes the prophet or seer if he chooses to undertake the long and arduous pilgrimage to eternal stature. Alternately he may feel called more to the immediate fellowship of a spiritual service here and now, and thus may give himself to full-time religious work.

Through the ages there is always the transcendental influence of the few who have affirmed a truth, and given it a personal dramatization until the spreading impact of their effort has created a new facet in the spiritual tradition. The great sagas of these avatars, or perhaps the less universal pioneers of faith, have been preserved in sacred scriptures of myriad form and content. The agonies and exaltations of the Great Ones in particular have come to be recreated over and over again, and thus have established an infinite variety of rituals. The Christian Eucharist is a familiar example. The origin of Sabian ceremonies and methods in the lives and works of Jesus, Ezekiel and the Babylonian Isaiah has been explained in the greatest detail.

In such rituals of higher self-discovery the least of men may have healing and regeneration, since in the religious experience they have made their own they share a reality with the spiritual giants who have gone before. This is the outreaching to the periphery of possible self-orientation. It is an almost paradoxical self-centering that has its effectiveness in the universality of the self-extension. For the moment man is all-man, or the totality of his fellows as well as himself. What in the operation of mind ramifies out from center, and is ordered through philosophy, is conversely and by the heart pulled in towards center as it is ordered by the senses and comes to be known as a manifestation of faith rather than reason. Religion, as the companion of philosophy, creates sympathy and good will as the complementation of understanding and insight. The religious exaltation or sustainment that brings men to their transcendental self-fulfillment in a sharing of immortal experience is a vital and constant revelation of human nature in its universal potential. The achievement of the ecstasy, and the accompanying sublimation of lower appetites and instincts, requires an uncompromising respect for personality in conjunction with the recognition of the integrity of experience on which an effective philosophy depends.

The all-important corollary realization is that it is in the individual's religious experience with all men collectively, whether in one fashion or another, that his relationship with God becomes a personal one. Through his own centering of the whole he gains the essential intimacy of any truly divine revelation, and thereupon rises above all the hopeless divisions and needlessly bitter competi-

tions of everyday living. He becomes the healer and the
mystic and indeed steward of everything that man may
embrace in his journey toward fulfillment under the
Solar Mysteries.

Here is the Sabian conception of a pure religion. The
aspirant who desires an immortal realization without the
need of any buttressing through reason or emotion must
accept the basic rightness of his own motives and impulses.
He must do this because the kingdom of heaven is within
him.

In achieving a religious life he must (1) recognize the
extent to which he creates his own actual reality by living
his days in the light of the truth he accepts for the centering of his effort and (2) see to it that this truth is an
exalted one. He learns to establish and hold in consciousness whatever he would have as the over-all pattern of
manifestation for himself and those around him. To his
study of man's commerce with ideas through the ages he
adds an interest and participation in a healing ministry,
in order that everything may be brought as far as possible
to the full of its potentials here and now. He is taught
to make his rehearsal of the past a blessing of the present
through the ritualization of his life under the Solar
Mysteries.

The Third Axiom

All mastery of all things is possible to all men. This
is the axiom of necessary initiative.

If philosophy is man's practical examination of his
ideas, and religion his ritualization of his aspiration,
science is his tireless and infinitely audacious multiplica-
tion and ramification of the skills with which he has en-

dowed himself. Science affords the means whereby he has wrought the miracles of modern technology, and thus has seemed to place even the planet itself in complete subjugation to his whim. He has made a cosmic responsibility very largely his own, and current history is almost wholly the account of his struggle to achieve by the genius of his own effort.

To the head and the heart must be added the hands, or the works of everyday responsibility as a basis for the individual's perspective on his well-being. Differing from thoughts that must always be brought to center in his own mind, or from emotional experiences that carry him to the periphery of his concern over his relationship with his fellows, the genius of his creative contributions is that they can be stood on their own foundation in a cancellation of all dependence on himself and thus and in a curious fashion be given a life of their own.

The construct set up by God, or by the man created in His image, is as much an organic entity as the organism endowed with life by nature. It has its own center as the gift of its creator, and its effectiveness is furthered by a proper respect for the independent frame of reference in which it operates. This is the commonplace accomplishment that in primitive times or to untutored minds seems to be the sheerest magic. Here the divinatory techniques on which occultism builds so largely in present days are of the greatest value through the training they give in establishing these constructs of reality, and in manipulating the time-and-space lattice so that the results of effort may be anticipated with confidence.

The seer becomes a counselor, and the dedicated individual a partner in worthy achievement. The present moment, whenever there is a clear view of the potential in all things, provides an unlimited and continuing opportunity. The seeker comes into his own through an initiative that owes nothing to anything other than itself, once he understands that he can be said to be ultimately and solely whatever he may find himself to be in the essence of his own existence. His fulfillment comprehends and so at will may actualize the absolute illimitability of which in potential he now is ever conscious in the depths of himself. Infinity and universality do not comprise limitations that he must accept but rather reveal the limitless transcendence of time and space within which his self-expression creates the concepts for its own ordering.

Here is the Sabian conception of a pure science, or of human consciousness released to the full manifestation of its own creative genius.

All things are seen as related to all other things, and in consequence they afford continuous signatures of a potentiality inherent in the immediateness of every time-and-space relationship. The mind may be guided and the heart stimulated at every point of effort and progress, but the initiative is of its own order and its own making and therefore invariable in its roots and branches. Outwardly and in material things this determination to action affords an evidence of itself in the extent and form of its mastery of the physical world.

Man in his works, no less than in his insights and in his innermost and actually inarticulate faith, may find himself forever both indomitable in his ongoing and infallible in his realization. It is through the honesty of his self-expression that he is able to resist the infinite regression away from the immediate union of himself and the universe for which and in which he acts. It is then that his life in its contribution to his world and his fellows becomes a living of all-life under the Solar Mysteries.

Summary

Man must make allowances for his presuppositions in every thought and action, but it is within his power to select whatever assumption best sustains him in his expression of himself. Philosophy is the means by which he orders life to his liking, through the functions of mind.

Man creates the actual reality in which he finds himself through the fundamental truth he accepts for the centering of his aspiration, and he reaches his spiritual fulfillment through a realization of the basic rightness of his motives and impulses. Religion is the means by which he rehearses his spiritual insights and thereby effects his ultimate reconciliation with his highest desire for himself.

Man exists most fundamentally in his works, or in his acts or reactions of being, and his arrival at any worthy stature is entirely a question of his creative accomplishment or of his service to his fellows and his world at large. Science is the means whereby he harnesses his skills in order to employ them in genuine creative fashion, and thereby achieve his ultimate potentiality.

The basis for any self-unfoldment under the Solar Mysteries is (1) an acceptance of the complete integrity of experience, (2) the culture of a genuine respect for all personality and (3) the development of an individual gift for utilizing the creative powers of consciousness.

All things are related to all other things, and the

realization of any relationship in any or all of its pertinent details is through philosophy, religion and science, that is, by means of thought, feeling and expended effort. Thinking provides experience with a center of reference, emotion gives experience a complementary periphery of reference and skill maintains the frame of reference for any particular detail of experience.

Knowledge is valid only through its continual verification in experience, and the verification is accomplished through an awareness of consequences and a recognition of analogy and probability. Knowledge has a reliable expansion only as single minds project it through the thinking of many minds. Precise definition of terms and accurate statement of fact and reaction constitute the underlying basis of dependable knowledge. Knowledge is defeated or limited only in (1) the acceptance of delimitations for the self as irrevocable and (2) the pursuit of infinite regressions of relationship away from the immediateness of actual experience.

Man manipulates the factors of experience in degrees of remove from himself by a use of ideas, and as these are brought into leash by the mind they are known as concepts. The Sabian project in consequence is sometimes identified as the philosophy of concepts.

Man comes to know God through the fulfillment of himself in religious experience, and when this becomes personal he is able to serve his fellows as the avatar-to-be or as a healing presence in everyday affairs.

In his creative initiative, and its immortal centering within his own potentials, the aspirant becomes the initiate and the glory of his kind.

STUDY GROUP

Call to order at announced hour of meeting

Welcome to visitors

INTONATION OF THE SACRED VOWELS

Leader

Father, let darkness depart;
Guard us from far-reaching harm;
Pardon our hardness of heart;
Bar every harbored alarm!

Ancient of Days, lift Thy face;
Blaze with unwavering flame;
Save us we pray through Thy grace;
Raise us by faith in Thy name!

Heal us, Redeemer Unseen;
Free us from needless ordeal;
Keep our hearts eager and clean;
Teach us to seek Thee with zeal!

Guide us, O Christ Crucified;
Bind all desire to Thy light;
Fire us to life magnified;
Find our ways right in Thy sight!

Holy Jehovah, bend low;
O Lord of Hosts, make us whole;
Hold our hearts close in Thy glow;
Know our devotion of soul!

Ruler Triune, grant us youth;
School us in beauty of mood;
Groom us in fruits of Thy truth;
Prove our faith truly renewed!

Indwelling Spirit, take wing;
Quicken a vigor of will;
Give us convictions that sing;
Lift us to infinite skill!

(THE MINOR VOWELS)

Call us in awe to Thy law;
Caution us all against flaw!

Spare us our wearing despair;
Share what we bear Thee in prayer!

Grant us Thy sanctified plan;
Band us for salvaging man!

Stop all our mocking of God:
Watch that we honor Thy rod!

Pledge us Thy strength in our quest,
Let all our stress come to rest!

Put us on footing more sure;
Look that our good shall endure!

Stir us to worship Thy word;
Further the search long deferred!

Justify us from above;
Suffer the flood of Thy love!

Point out all toil to avoid;
Join us in joy unalloyed!

Rouse us, O rout every doubt;
Now let Thy vowels speak out!

Exposition and discussion

(On Monday evenings particularly)

BENEDICTION OF THE ELEMENTS

Leader

May the fountain of the waters of life
    Spring eternal within you!
May the breath of the Spirit
    Consecrate the cloister of your heart!
May you truly be child of earth,
    Living to nourish the seed of the word!
And may the cosmic fire rise
    Forever torchlike through your being!

(On Wednesday evenings particularly)

Admonition to the Senses

Leader

> May your eyes be blind to evil
> That your sight be opened within!
> May your ears be deaf to discord
> That you hear celestial strains!
> May your tongue rest silent in stress
> That your words carry spiritual power!
> May your nostrils ignore every stench
> That you catch the fragrance of Eden!
> And may your fingers be fearless of thorn
> That the flowers in your garden be roses!

HEALING RITUAL

EVOCATION ON THE STEPS

Leader

> Bind us whose souls are outreaching;
> Mold us who search for the best;
> Blind us to profitless teaching;
> Hold us to greatness of quest!
>
> Open our eyes to our mission,
> Step number one, in rebirth
> Held through inspired ambition,
> Drawing sustainment from earth,
>   Thanking God for the joy of its worth!

In unison

> Bind us whose souls are outreaching;
> Mold us who search for the best;
> Blind us to profitless teaching;
> Hold us to greatness of quest!

Leader

> Open our nostrils to spirit,
> Step number two, in appeal
> Inward to faith lest we fear it,
> Finding new strength in ordeal,
>   Seeking fullness in creative zeal!

In unison

> Bind us whose souls are outreaching;

Mold us who search for the best;
Blind us to profitless teaching;
Hold us to greatness of quest!

Leader

Open our lips to decision,
Step number three, in new light
Brought when the law kindles vision,
Showing that worship is right,
Lifting man to his place in God's sight!

In unison

Bind us whose souls are outreaching;
Mold us who search for the best;
Blind us to profitless teaching;
Hold us to greatness of quest!

Leader

Open our ears to God's leading,
Step number four, in fresh view
Gained as we hear the heart's pleading,
Realizing what we can do,
Making insight eternally true!

In unison

Bind us whose souls are outreaching;
Mold us who search for the best;
Blind us to profitless teaching;
Hold us to greatness of quest!

Leader

Open our hands to real giving,
Step number five, in high need
Always to bless life in living,
Cleansing our souls of all greed,
Proving service a magic indeed!

In unison

Bind us whose souls are outreaching;
Mold us who search for the best;
Blind us to profitless teaching;
Hold us to greatness of quest!

Leader

Open our minds to reflection,
Step number six, in desire
Held to no less than perfection,
Sharing the truth we inspire,
Thanking God for the signs we require!

In unison

Bind us whose souls are outreaching;
Mold us who search for the best;
Blind us to profitless teaching;
Hold us to greatness of quest!

Leader

Open our hearts to God's healing,
Step number seven, in skill
Born of compassionate feeling,
Strengthening action in will,
Letting faith come to rest and be still!

In unison

Bind us whose souls are outreaching;
Mold us who search for the best;
Blind us to profitless teaching;
Hold us to greatness of quest!

PREFATORY ACKNOWLEDGMENT

Leader

We acknowledge that to receive we only have to ask,

and that to have the entire celestial realm of perfect consummation opened unto us we only have to knock, and we affirm that through our invisible fellowship we approach the door of the silence that awaits our touch and admits us on the manifestation of our faith and appreciation.

Healing silence

Consummatory Acknowledgment
Leader

We acknowledge the presence of a healing power which we know to be of God, and all that we have been unable to use here constructively we now release and send forth into the Universal for the blessing of every soul to whom it may be given.

Consecration to the Indwelling Spirit
Leader

We consecrate our hearts to Thee;
From bonds of sense we must be free—
In answer comes the whisper clear,
Be still, and know that love is here!

We consecrate our worldly all
And place it subject to Thy call—
Soft comes the voice from higher sphere,
Be still, and know that wealth is here!

We consecrate our thought and mind
To spread Thy word to all mankind—

The inner answer seems so near,
Be still, and know that peace is here!

We consecrate our depths of soul
To furthering Thy blessed goal—
    The answer is in every ear,
    Be still, and know that hope is here!

MEDITATION ON THE HEALING GIFTS

Leader
Be still, and know that love is here!
    A divinely all-embracing love,
    A healing, sustaining love,
    The love of a heavenly father for his children,
    The love of a child for its parents,
    The love of loved ones, one for another—
This divinely-appointed healing love is here—
    Be still!

Be still, and know that wealth is here!
    A practical, spendable and manifest wealth,
    A wealth of this world created by and for this world,
    A wealth that aids complete and tangible self-expression,
    A wealth that an envoy of the Spirit should possess,
    A wealth as lower sign of a higher mastery of values—
This divinely-appointed sustaining wealth is here!
    Be still!

Be still, and know that peace is here!
    A quiet indwelling peace,
    A perfect satisfying peace,

A peace that lies deep within the very depths of being,
A peace that leads to the joyous outreaching of self,
A peace that is the sole and only source of happiness—
This divinely-appointed exalting peace is here!
    Be still!

Be still, and know that hope is here!
    A hope that leads to every proper expression of self,
    A hope that closes firmly the door to the past,
    A hope that opens wide the gateway to the future,
    A hope that gives point and purpose to all experience,
    A hope that leads to understanding—
This divinely-appointed enlightening hope is here!
    Be still!

HEALING DISMISSAL

Leader

May the temple of your living flesh
Be worthy of your high desire;
May your worldly place in daily life
Bring recompense in rich degree;
May your happiness and state of heart
Endear you everywhere you go;
And may the spirit stirring deep within
Be ever-conscious in your thoughts!

CHAPEL SERVICE

(Opens with healing ritual, omitting healing dismissal and continuing uninterruptedly)

SABIAN DOXOLOGY

In Unison

> Praise God to Whom my heart would be
>> Upraised through all eternity;
> Praise God that I where'er I go
>> Through all my life my God shall know!

Devotional address, inspirational program or prefatory remarks in connection with a dedication

(If offering is taken)

BLESSING OF THE OFFERING

Leader

> Mother Earth, do grant to us
>> The sharing of Thy substance;
> Father Sky, we ask that this our offering be lifted up
>> Unto the measure of our love for Thee;
> Sister Water, may we now know through Thee
>> The full and perfect flow of Thy prosperity;
> Brother Fire, may we within be kindled
>> In the flaming glory of our gift of self!

Silent ritual for receipt of offering

Ritual of affirmation

SABIAN AFFIRMATIONS
(For health, prosperity and happiness in order)

In unison

(First fortnight)
I rely on the healing power of God within me.
I enter every experience with the whole of myself.
My heart has found the shrine at every wayside.

(Second fortnight)
I am the temple of the illimitable now.
I build new sense of values every day.
My joys are fresh-created from on high.

(Third fortnight)
My body is the treasure house of higher thoughts.
I bring new life to everything in which I participate.
I welcome every phase of life within my soul.

(Fourth fortnight)
I recognize God's purpose in every phase of life.
My wealth is based upon the joy of service.
I live today in gratitude for yesterday.

(Fifth fortnight)
My being is enlarged in my constancy of faith.
I dedicate my world to God in every thought and act.
I thrill within my heart to every breath of life.

(Sixth fortnight)
I bring the whole of myself to dwell in lasting peace.
Whatever I take from life I accept as high responsibility.
My soul is lighted at the flame of unceasing aspiration.

(Seventh fortnight)
I consecrate every interest of my life to higher values.
My efforts are repaid through the indwelling presence.
I dwell within the joy of an eternal revelation.

(Eighth fortnight)
I yield my heart and soul and mind to some exalted task.
The higher manifestations in my life I share with all.
My house within has endless room for godly guests.

(Ninth fortnight)
I seek constructive use for all I draw to me.
The goods for which I strive are of eternal worth.
My heart is opened wide to every song of life.

(Tenth fortnight)
I reconsecrate my soul to my divine indwelling.
My fortune has its root in the eternal now.
I find immortal signatures no matter where I am.

(Eleventh fortnight)
I welcome every challenge to my higher understanding.
A full supply for here and now is my divine inheritance.
My soul is forever nourished by its own enduring source.

(Twelfth fortnight)
Within myself I seek to mirror the perfect all.
I lift the turmoil of the day to greater harmony.
My soul is linked to all of life in ever-higher ties.

(*Thirteenth fortnight*)

My being is the shrine of indwelling light and love.
My riches have their source in God's abundance.
I now have found the sunshine of divine compassion.

(*Fourteenth fortnight*)

I enter the temple of self with reverence.
I meet the life of everyday with never-ceasing interest.
My inner self responds to every outer joy.

(*Fifteenth fortnight*)

Within my body the healing peace of God abides.
My ambitions are sustained in the highest realization.
I am free from bondage to the world of transient things.

(*Sixteenth fortnight*)

I see perfection manifest here and now.
The world responds to my endless faith in its promise.
My heart renews its fellowship with every other heart.

(*Seventeenth fortnight*)

I know within myself the law of God and good.
There is profit in every channel of my effort.
In all my joys I seek an added richness.

(*Eighteenth fortnight*)

I hearken to the voice of higher values.
My wealth is manifest within myself.
My soul is charged with vibrant joy from everywhere.

(*Nineteenth fortnight*)

My body is my soul's real dwelling place.
I give a heightened recompense for all I ask in life.
I see the smile of God in every passing face.

(Twentieth fortnight)
I welcome God to every corner of my heart.
I find new use for every inner resource.
The joys I know are shared by all the world.

(Twenty-first fortnight)
I shape my temple to divine desire.
I share the wealth of every other person.
My heart receives the truth from every source.

(Twenty-second fortnight)
I perfect myself within the frame of highest expectation.
I am the master of my circumstances.
My soul rejoices in the good that comes to others.

(Twenty-third fortnight)
My outer being is reborn within.
I dwell within the sunshine of the Presence.
My spirit claims the fellowship of greater values.

(Twenty-fourth fortnight)
I make myself essential to the flow of outer life.
I use my wealth to give it life and power.
My heart re-echoes peace from every heart.

(Twenty-fifth fortnight)
I thrill anew to cosmic love and harmony.
I acknowledge the infinity of resource.
There is no joy in which I do not share.

(Twenty-sixth fortnight)
Within myself the perfect plan is born.
I recognize new worth in everything I touch.
I give the world a fellowship of faith.

Leader

> May the love and wealth, the peace and hope
> Of the Indwelling Spirit
> > Dwell within you
> > Consciously
> > Forever!
> Amen!

DEDICATION CEREMONIES

(Chapel service precedes, with affirmations and benediction omitted. C signifies celebrant, Q questioner, U in unison, I individual respondent.)

C: Now let us bring our consciousness to the spiritual task at hand.

Q: How do we bring our consciousness to a spiritual task?

C: By realizing our oneness in the higher desire we are sharing at this moment.

Q: Are we not always at one in our spiritual reality?

C: True enough! Our basic atoneness is our eternal and universal being. However, our individual or effective identity, both in spirit and in lower or everyday manifestation, has its actuality in the immediate interest and purpose to which we give ourselves.

Q: Cannot the interest and purpose to which we give ourselves be self-seeking, and so be wholly unworthy?

C: When our self-seeking is individual in the sense of something separative, or something sought apart from our fellows, it becomes destructive and indeed most unworthy. But when it is held in common, with all who may care to have a part in its objectives and rewards, it is then an example of that cosmic division of labor through which each of us is able to develop his true personality.

Q: Is it in true personality, seen as a proper distinction from each other, that we should bring our consciousness to the spiritual task?

C: Yes, since it is in the fellowship of this contribution of distinctive realization from each of us that we are able to bring our higher and common desire to fulfillment.

Q: The achievement of a spiritual task is the fulfillment of a higher and common desire?

C: Necessarily! Only then do we achieve our conscious at-one-ment. But the consummation of the spiritual task is also a practical matter because it facilitates an individual dedication, and sustains a genuinely personal service as a special and vicarious fulfillment of some less developed facet of aspiration for each of the others in our invisible fellowship.

Q: And to what spiritual task are we asked now to bring our consciousness?

(Questions and responses continue uninterruptedly through the ceremonial part proper for the occasion.)

Part One: The Dedication of a Life

C: Our task is the dedication of this child *(these children, this seeker, these seekers)* to the vision of the Solar Mysteries.

Q: Why should this child *(these children, this seeker, these seekers)* be dedicated to the vision of the Solar Mysteries?

C: To the end that his *(her, their)* consciousness may have its channelship in his *(her, their)* very highest potentiality.

Q: How will he *(she, they)* know that this channelship is real?

C: By (1) his *(her, their)* conscious and constant fellowship with the great souls of all the ages, whether in intimate actuality or in wholly symbolical fashion, by (2) his *(her, their)* continual sense of participation in the great works of the race, whether modestly or in some truly responsible degree, and by (3) his *(her, their)* unswerving faithfulness to the chosen ritualizations of his *(her, their)* inner desire through the Sabian or other presentation of the Solar Mysteries.

Q: What is required of him *(her, them)* as his *(her, their)* part in this moment of his *(her, their)* dedication?

C: A lifting of his *(her, their)* consciousness to an apex of aspiration, so that this level of self-realization may be established for his *(her, their)* reassurance forever in this moment of orientation through his *(her, their)* spiritually-minded fellows here assembled, and so that in consequence it never thereafter will be necessary in times of stress or discouragement for this self-realization to drop to any lower level of manifestation.

Q: If the one *(ones)* to be dedicated be a child *(children)* in years or in understanding of these things pertaining to the Solar Mysteries, how will he *(she, they)* be able to lift his *(her, their)* consciousness effectively?

C: Any or all of those present for the performance of the spiritual task will lift the consciousness of such a one *(ones)* for him *(her, them)* in the actuality of spiritual fellowship as it is brought to atoneness in this moment of shared self-heightening. And if the reaffirmation of these principles has had a proper attention from all here

present, and if the one *(ones)* to be dedicated is *(are)* now
ready, let us proceed to the Ceremony of Water or the
alchemical adoration of the element of pure experience.

Q: Is this Ceremony of Water like the baptism of the
Christian church? Are we participating in a sacrament
that we can believe will have the power or authority to
cleanse from sin? Are we undertaking to endorse sponsors
for the spiritual upbringing or instruction of the child
too young or the seeker too inexperienced to affirm for
himself?

C: Yes, we are doing both, but with an occult or
strictly psychological rather than ecclesiastical orientation.
The ceremony is in no way designed to meet the requirements of any church for the baptism of its adherents, and
under the Solar Mysteries the aspirant as his own ultimate
sponsor must himself confirm his dedication at every
opportunity.

Q: Isn't there an occult or psychological cleansing
from sin in this Ceremony of Water?

C: That is true, certainly, but it is a self-cleansing that
follows from the conscious repudiation of sin as possessing
any sort of necessity or compulsion in the seeker's life.

Q: Then the seeker on the path is free from sin?

C: He remains himself in every natural respect, and
so he will continue to experience his lesser impulses. But
now he will know that they are unimportant, and as he
realizes their growing inconsequence in his everyday experience he will find them less and less a factor in his
being.

Q: And so there is no escape from one's own nature,
no matter how ill-developed or unlovely?

C: There is rather an exaltation of one's own nature, with all its ill-development and unloveliness, since it is within one's self that everyone at last and in truth must find himself. Therefore it is wise to turn within for strength in any significant moment of life, and with that in mind let us be silent and turn within and give ourselves every opportunity to reflect on these things.

Silence for reflection

C: And now let us stand and take our places in the presence of this water! In our alchemical adoration of this most liquid of the elements, we enlist its powers for the consummation of our ceremony.

U: We acknowledge the waters of life as our living sustainment. We acknowledge the purity of source in every human experience. We acknowledge the sustaining fellowship of the immortals in all our aspiration. We acknowledge our cleansing of soul through the heightened consciousness of this moment. And out of the eternal ocean of potentiality we dedicate this child *(these children, this seeker, these seekers)* to the highest manifestation of his *(her, their)* immortal being.

I: I, *(in turn each one so dedicated naming himself in full),* accept and welcome this dedication of myself to my higher potentiality, and I recognize that after such dedication there is no turning back. I give eternal thanks to all who here have participated in thus dedicating my life.

OR: I, for *(naming in full a child or individual unable to speak up for himself),* accept and welcome this dedication of himself *(herself)* to his *(her)* higher potentiality, and for myself I, *(naming himself in full),* accept the responsibility for helping him *(her)* understand that after such dedication there is no turning back. I shall encourage him *(her)* to give eternal thanks to all who have had part in thus dedicating his *(her)* life.

I: I, *(in turn each person not accepting dedication but participating in the ceremony naming himself in full),* rededicate myself in this moment of assisting in your dedication, *(naming in full each of those so dedicated),* and I pledge the fullest of invisible fellowship with you.

C: Now let us be seated.

Dismissal at Dedication

Celebrant

> May God hold sacred
>> What we have here pledged;
> May man hold hallowed
>> What has now been set apart on high;
> May all enlightenment on lower planes
>> Sustain this dedication;
> And may the dedicated vision
>> Serve the hopes of all humanity!

Part Two: The Dedication of a Departure

C: Our task is the dedication of a life brought to its conclusion in earthly and bodily terms, to the end that its living may be continued as an immortal contribution under the Solar Mysteries.

Q: But has not the contribution already been made?

C: Reality is not subject to the clock and never need come to a stop in time. It exists in its own continuance, or as it remains a living factor in human experience.

Q: But when one of our company passes at length to the grave?

C: The grave is an end to the body, but not to immortal embodiment.

Q: Isn't the afterlife in another and entirely different sort of world?

C: There is but one world under God, and there are few indeed who are able to experience God's, world in its oneness. It is because of those who fail in this that we have our conceptions of heaven and hell, and of an actuality of separation.

Q: Then there is a practical significance of the Biblical statement, that the kingdom of heaven is within us?

C: Everything is within us in an ultimate sense. However, it is as we experience things outwardly, or in the everyday reality we share and identify as a lower world of manifestation, that we possess them for ourselves or in the separateness of bodily identity.

Q: Then why should we dedicate a life when it no longer is any part of the world of manifestation where we know it, or where we know ourselves and it knows itself?

C: Our dedication facilitates an experience of personal immortality, or a transcendence of the limitations of birth and death.

Q: An experience of personal immortality for our deceased companion, or for ourselves?

C: Both. The one who has come to the grave has

lived in the events of his lifetime, and has developed his
everyday personality through his acts and reactions in connection with them. As we hold these warm in memory,
and give them a dramatic continuity such as can linger
in the minds of men, we are continuing the reality in
which he has had his being. In that fashion he is immortal in a true personal sense, and continues on among
us.

Q: In a conscious awareness on his part?

C: With no difference in his self-awareness except
that, lacking a body, he is limited to sharing the experience brought to focus in the bodies of those with whom
he is linked in significant living.

Q: How many of us can count on doing things significant enough to sustain us in a bodiless state when we
in turn have passed on, or can count on being worthy
enough to be memorialized in this way?

C: In our invisible fellowship our very least participation is a contribution to its ongoing, and in some ways
the greatest contribution is the faithfulness of a consciousness and a devotion that may have had very little
outer form.

Q: Can we dedicate anything as intangible as that?

C: In our moment of grief, when the time comes to
dismiss the body of a dear one among us to the physical
grave, we can etch his love and warmth into our common consciousness and thus retain them as the very essence of immortal fellowship.

Q: And etching them in that manner has meaning to
him, consciously?

C: All the meaning in the world. Through our etching of his essential reality in our common being in this way he is afforded the continuance of the living he has known with us, and this makes it possible for him to become one of the invisible workers responsible for so much of our spiritual strength as a group under the Solar Mysteries.

Q: Does that mean that the experience of personal immortality, for those of us left incarnate in our own flesh, is through our own and similar awareness of this strength in the group?

C: All that and much more, since the contact with the deceased can be quite personal and in some respects as tangible as anything else in life.

Q: Is this the explanation of spiritual visitations, and of the many forms of contact with exalted and unembodied personalities?

C: No general explanations are possible when it comes to things of spiritual dimension, but there is no mystery about superphysical experiences except as they are made mysterious by human minds.

Q: Then death is not really a mystery?

C: As has been said so beautifully by Wordsworth, our birth into the flesh is but a sleep and a forgetting. And when death comes among those who like us are engaged in a spiritual service to mankind we can rededicate such a heightened living in a dimension greater than the time-and-space focus of trial and stress, and thereupon we can find that the sleep has but prepared us for the conscious regrasping of the trailing glory our souls have brought from afar for its sharing, and that the forgetting at last has been made impossible in the love we sustain through our invisible fellowship. And with these things in mind, and if the reaffirmation of the principles has had a proper attention from all here present and if the one who will speak for the deceased is ready, let us proceed to the Ceremony of Earth or the alchemical adoration of the element of ultimate consequences.

Q: Is this Ceremony of Earth designed to provide the same assurance of immortality as is offered in the church and fraternal funeral services?

C: The funeral services of the churches and fraternal orders are the most proper of assurances in the light of their teachings and practices, and of necessity the same may be expected of us in our presentation of the Solar Mysteries.

Q: Do we differ from them very greatly then, when we dedicate the life of someone deceased among us to a conscious continuance and so ultimately to a greater self-fulfillment?

C: We are not seeking to make death tolerable by balancing an assurance of afterworld compensation, or of rewards remote in our experience, against a present finality in the event. Rather we dramatize an expanded or exalted living such as transcends any and all accident of external consequences.

Q: Just how does our ceremony dramatize this?

C: The ceremony permits us to dedicate to a continual living what the deceased has been contributing to our common consciousness, and in this memorial moment of heightened fellowship at the time of outer transition on his (*her*) part we recreate the drama of our immortal sustainment in each other.

Q: Then we must continue to hold him (*her*) in mind consciously?

C: There is no need for any fixity of obligation such as soon can become a burden. In this our dedication we contribute to his (*her*) continuing incarnation in our common ongoing, and in it also we re-establish the immortality of our fellowship and thus make possible his (*her*) eventual return among us in some new fullness of the vision he (*she*) has held. And since it is within us that he (*she*) must have his (*her*) contact now, let us be silent and give him (*her*) every opportunity to make his (*her*) presence known to us while we reflect on these things.

Silence for reflection

C: And now let us stand in full appreciation for the substance of the outer world here hallowed in memory of the departed! In our alchemical adoration of this most plastic of the elements, we enlist its powers for the consummation of our ceremony.

U: We acknowledge the integrity of nature in its embodiment of all our works. We acknowledge the certainty of consequences in all our conscious experience. We acknowledge the magic of the seed we may plant precisely as we wish in the days of our incarnation. We acknowledge the nourishing of our soul through the deepening of our consciousness and its ramification through the earth. And out of the history of man etched across the face of our globe we commemorate the physical life of (*naming the deceased in full*) and dedicate his (*her*) memory for the immortal ongoing we may share with him (*her*) in every deeper and broader dimension of reality.

I: I, for (*the one assigned to speak for the deceased naming the deceased in full*), accept the dedication of his (*her*) memory in the highest immortalization of his (*her*) vision.

I: I, (*in turn each other participant in the ceremony naming himself in full*), rededicate myself in this moment of commemoration of the life and work of (*naming the deceased in full*) and pledge myself to do my part in keeping him (*her*) present among us in the pursuit of our common vision.

C: Now let us be seated.

DISMISSAL AT DEDICATION

Celebrant

> May God hold sacred
>   What we have here pledged;
> May man hold hallowed
>   What has now been set apart on high;
> May all enlightenment on lower planes
>   Sustain this dedication;
> And may the dedicated vision
>   Serve the hopes of all humanity!

PART THREE: THE DEDICATION OF A PARTNERSHIP

C: Our task is the dedication of these souls in the special intimacy they are prepared to share, to the end that it may be worthy of the Solar Mysteries.

Q: Why should their special intimacy be worthy of the Solar Mysteries?

C: Because through it and together they each may develop the personality of depth and scope they would be unable to develop alone.

Q: In what way will their special intimacy make this possible?

C: Because each in his partner has a constant added facet for his own being, and so is multiplied in the effectiveness of his self-refinement.

Q: Would this not result from any normal close association with others?

C: Normal close association does not have the irrevocability required by the Solar Mysteries. What is added to self on immortal levels must be without any possibility of a cancellation or a turning back. Relationships that are Solar in nature must be both eternal in ongoing and universal in their mutual self-fulfillment.

Q: Can irrevocability of such a sort have any actual merit in a world of chance and change?

C: When we project ourselves out of the superficial realms of chance and change, on up and into an immortal reality, we must create the eternality and universality we ask for our larger freedom by establishing it in the widening limitations needed for sustainment through every lesser relationship.

Q: Is that the familiar paradox that in any partnership the surrender of petty privileges is the price of the more rewarding ones?

C: Irrevocable surrenders are the basis of all true dependability, and they must be of all-sweeping scope if a special intimacy is to be dedicated to the Solar Mysteries.

Q: Such a partnership then must be supreme above and beyond all others?

C: An aspirant is expected to be faithful to every partnership he forms, whether business or political or marital, and as a seeker under the Solar Mysteries he must complete the cycle of each of these to the uttermost of his capacity. However and at the same time it is his right as a matter of free choice to make any one of these central in his spiritual aspiration. As he does so he may ask that the particular partnership have a special dedication, and in that ritualized recognition be set more significantly at the forefront of his inner orientation.

Q: But when it comes to a choice in human partnerships, is not marriage the most important?

C: Not necessarily. Many great souls throughout history have adopted celibacy for their course. And much more importantly, we must never lose sight of the fact that general rules for spiritual values are quite impossible.

Q: The course of the celibates in some cases is then the better one? Is nonindulgence of the senses perhaps the best of all ways of spiritual enlightenment?

C: The disciplines of sense restraint have been taught since time immemorial in numberless occult and religious systems, and they have their value in strengthening the seeker's will. Nonetheless their practical result is all too often the seeker's progressive withdrawal from the everyday experience of his fellows, and thereupon and in consequence a spiritual self-destruction.

Q: The implication then is that under the Solar Mysteries we should strive for a greater rather than a lesser participation in human experience?

C: That is right. We seek to follow the divine example, and we belive that God ever participates in even the least activity of His creation.

Q: Then our partnerships should be for the purpose of increasing our participation in human experience?

C: Correct! And since the mating insight is at the very core of the integrity of the race, at least on the levels of visible manifestation, a necessary refinement of this built-in priority of the racial consciousness makes marriage a natural first choice for a basic partnership and therefore provides the form most commonly seeking its dedication under the Solar Mysteries.

Q: What if another form of partnership has been dedicated, and a participant comes to consider marriage and look for its dedication?

C: Anyone once dedicated to partnership is forever so dedicated, and all possible ramification of his relations with his fellows will be found to fit happily and richly into this one and only primary ordering of his intimacies.

Q: What happens when a partner deceases?

C: All relationships given their seal under the Solar Mysteries lie far above the vicissitudes of time-and-space complexity. In consequence no imagination can conjure up contingencies for which the Solar priorities are not a rewarding solution. If the kingdom of heaven is held firmly, everything else falls into place very promptly. And if the reaffirmation of these principles has had a proper attention from all here present, and if the souls asking for dedication of their special intimacy are ready, let us proceed to the Ceremony of Fire or the alchemical adoration of the element of pure existence.

Q: Does this Ceremony of Fire correspond to the performance of a marriage ceremony by a priest or minister or magistrate?

C: There is some parallel, but the dedication is not necessarily of the marital relationship and it is in no way designed to serve as the religious or civil ceremony required by law or social custom.

Q: Is there an essential difference between this Ceremony of Fire and the ceremony by which a clergyman or civil officer unites a man and a woman so that they can be said to be of one flesh?

C: The institution of marriage in society provides primarily for a legitimacy of offspring and an adjudication of property rights, and it tends very effectively to idealize romance and to discourage profligacy. Under the Solar Mysteries the dedication of the special intimacy is a practical means for expanding personal potentials in an eternally organic function, or a lifting rather than a licensing of the instincts and appetites and a consequent furthering of the social good through vision rather than law.

Q: The Ceremony of Fire accomplishes this?

C: It dedicates the creative fire at source, or deep within the being.

Q: But the special intimacy is a merging of outer interest and effort?

C: The intimacy becomes the visible sign of the inner dedication, which of itself will be known ultimately in its transcendental fulfillment. As a result of the outer dedication the divine fire is brought continually to the highest point of personal quickening of which the partners are capable at each stage of their unfoldment. And since this is sacred with them, that is, never an outward manifestation, let us be silent and reflect on these things to the end that our realization may facilitate the great alchemy these souls will come to know increasingly in their spiritual binding to each other.

Silence for reflection

C: And now let us stand in the presence of this holy flame as these souls clasp hands and seal their eternal commitment to each other. In our alchemical adoration of this most refining of the elements, we enlist its powers for the consummation of our ceremony.

U: We acknowledge the radiant energy built into the core of all conscious individuality. We acknowledge the creative drive through which the quickened heart may bring an incandescent interest to all experience. We acknowledge our illimitable capacity for an upflaming loyalty to obligations and convictions. We acknowledge our continual rebirth through the struggle of our aspiration to express itself. And out of the endless fructification of all reality we dedicate (*naming those so dedicated in full*) to the common destiny they have chosen for themselves under the Solar Mysteries.

I: I, (*in turn each of those dedicated naming himself or herself in full*), accept this dedication of myself and (*naming the partner or partners in full*) to our new and common destiny, and I recognize that after such dedication there is no turning back. I give my eternal thanks to all here who have participated in this dedication of the special intimacy we seek to make worthy of the Solar Mysteries.

I: I, (*in turn each other person participating in the ceremony naming himself in full*), rededicate myself in this moment of participation with you (*naming those dedicated in full*), in the dedication of your special intimacy, and I pledge the fullest of invisible fellowship with you in your common effort.

C: Now let us be seated.

DISMISSAL AT DEDICATION

Celebrant

> May God hold sacred
>   What we have here pledged;
> May man hold hallowed
>   What has now been set apart on high;
> May all enlightenment on lower planes
>   Sustain this dedication;
> And may the dedicated vision
>   Serve the hopes of all humanity!

PART FOUR: THE DEDICATION OF A PROJECT

C: Our task is the dedication of this (*naming project*) to the end that it may serve the Solar Mysteries through (*making a clear statement of the ideal to be furthered*).

Q: In what way will the (*naming project*) serve the Solar Mysteries?

C: In the fact that its purposes will be oriented to an ongoing superior to any limitation of time, and to a breadth of application beyond any limitation of space.

Q: How does the dedication help accomplish this?

C: By a repudiation of any necessary or ultimate limitation either in the continuing effort of the individual *(persons)* who seeks *(seek)* this dedication or in the vision that leads him *(her, them)* to this expenditure of himself *(herself, themselves)* and of his *(her, their)* means.

Q: Should not he *(she, they)* be dedicated, rather than the vision to be embodied in this *(naming project)?*

C: It is in common effort that spiritual aspiration gains its substance in experience, and the facilities of the objective world that may be dedicated to higher ends are of special value to the individual *(persons)* in an ordering and strengthening of his *(her, their)* efforts.

Q: Then it is wise for any activity of spiritual seeking such as a church or an occult group to have its dedicated temples, schools, libraries and everything of the sort?

C: Buildings and physical equipment, meetings and forms of organization, rituals and procedures, and the like are nothing of themselves. But when any of these are dedicated for an end through which spiritual aspirations are brought to creative unity, the participating individual is *(individuals are)* lifted above the time-and-space definition and his *(her, their)* immortal personality is *(personalities are)* able to dramatize itself *(themselves)* for the sake of others in the facilities through which the dedicated project serves the larger vision.

Q: A temple can be empty or effort without soul?

C: The creations and works of men are in any

spiritual reality the continuing beauty of the love and talent and genius built into their substance. But when these actually quite artificial entities demand the sacrifice of human beings and human resources for no more than perpetuating their outer shell, they become a mockery of the vision from which they have sprung.

Q: If our own lives are dedicated, rather than our projects, are we not better able to help maintain the spiritual vigor of our creations and our works?

C: That will always seem to be the more simple course, but it is only half the story. As we dedicate also the channels of our common effort we share a larger dedication as well, and then we have begun to be something more than ourselves alone. This is true even if we should achieve a status little short of an avatar at core.

Q: If our common effort centers in an organization of like-minded seekers, rather than in physical buildings and equipment, do we not give greater aid to our aspiration?

C: It makes no difference what the agency of facilitation may be, provided we may dedicate it to our common aspirations.

Q: If the dedication of facilities for our spiritual service is in this way so great a help to our increasing usefulness under the Solar Mysteries, should we not try to create some wonderful edifice or establish some great organization?

C: The source of any aspiration we serve is within us always, and so never in the outer and even splendid things through which it may be stimulated to an almost illimitable projection of itself. Whenever a dedicated place or organization proves to be beyond the capacity of the faithful who dedicate it to find it actually dramatizing their spiritual vision for them, or strengthening them in the course of their daily effort to live their vision and share it, such a place or organization at once loses its higher meaning. Thereupon it can only serve to depreciate everything of eternal worth.

Q: Is this the reason little of physical facility or organization is encouraged under the Solar Mysteries?

C: Under the Solar Mysteries we find our aspiration mirrored in the great invisible temple not made with hands. Hence in the practical world of everyday we utilize whatever facilities are most suitable for the immediate ends to which we can dedicate them, and these facilities we endow with every beauty and efficiency in our power without ever making them themselves a goal or losing ourselves in self-justification or superficial self-glorification in our attention to them. And if the reaffirmation of these principles has had a proper attention from all here present, and if the one *(ones)* among us who will offer the *(naming project)* for dedication are ready, let us proceed to the Ceremony of Air or the alchemical adoration of the element of ultimate realization.

Q: Is this Ceremony of Air the equivalent of the dedication ceremonies of the practical world around us?

C: The Ceremony of Air under the Solar Mysteries is in its largest expression the ministry of poetry, music and the arts, or the free capacity of man both to endow the world with a significance of his own choosing and to dramatize such a significance with a beauty his fellows will be able to appreciate.

Q: When we dedicate a *(naming project)* we are certifying an endowment of significance?

C: We are strengthening a practical ideal that in its exactions will be a continual reminder to man that he is a living and experimenting creature, rather than an automaton. We are confronting him with something to be done, and also and necessarily with a something he can do without thought of limitation to block him. This is so because dedication always certifies the possible.

Q: How will the dedication of this *(naming project)* certify these possible things to this seeker *(these seekers)?*

C: The *(naming project)* will become his *(her, their)* living embodiment in terms of a function now stabilized through the Solar Mysteries. The *(naming project)* is not dedicated to put him *(her, them)* in bondage to an obligation, but rather is to release him *(her, them)* in the terms of his *(her, their)* potentiality. And since his *(her, their)* release will be from within, let us be silent that we may sense some of the promise of this *(naming project)* and help dedicate it no less inwardly than outwardly.

Silence for reflection

C: And now let us stand in the presence of the eternal breath or immortal spirit that forever works silently and surely for the vivification of every eternal promise. In the alchemical adoration of this most pervading of the elements, we enlist its powers for the consummation of our ceremony.

U: We acknowledge the deep-seated restlessness of the human spirit in its endless aspiration. We acknowledge the necessity of constant change and growth as we develop our inner and ultimate orientations. We acknowledge the continual and conscious rehearsal of our experience as a basis for ultimate reality. We acknowledge our discipline of soul through the ceaseless interweaving of our ties with others. And out of the prodigal self-expenditure of all mankind through the ages we dedicate this *(naming project)* to the furthering of every possible accomplishment under the Solar Mysteries.

I: I, *(the sponsor for the project, or each sponsor in turn, naming himself or herself in full),* accept and welcome this dedication of *(naming project)* and of its function under the Solar Mysteries. I give eternal thanks to all who have participated in dedicating this vision.

I: I, *(in turn each other person participating in the ceremony naming himself or herself in full),* rededicate myself in this moment of participation in the dedication of this *(naming project)* and I pledge the fullest of invisible co-operation with the ends envisioned.

C: Now let us be seated.

DISMISSAL AT DEDICATION

Celebrant

> May God hold sacred
>   What we have here pledged;
> May man hold hallowed
>   What has now been set apart on high;
> May all enlightenment on lower planes
>   Sustain this dedication;
> And may the dedicated vision
>   Serve the hopes of all humanity!

FOR PRIVATE DEVOTIONS

GRACE TO THE ELEMENTS

Mother Earth, we thank Thee for Thy nutriment;
Father Sky, we thank Thee for Thy gift of
    discrimination in our food of every realm;
Sister Water, flow through us in fellowship
    as we two or more are gathered here;
Brother Fire, light our candles of the spirit
    that we may now ensoul the substance here received!

PRAYER OF PARTING ADORATION

    As I descend this mount, O Flame
      Follow me, and burn within!
    As I return to earth, O Breath,
      Quicken me, and dwell within!
    As I cede ecstasy, O God,
      Cherish me, and draw within!
    O Flame, O Breath, O God,
      I worship thee, I worship thee!

FULL MOON CEREMONY

*(C signifies celebrant, Q questioner, L legate, A acolyte,
N neophyte, U in unison)*

Unannounced preparatory silence

INVOCATION TO THE LIVING FLAME
Celebrant

> O Flame, we invoke Thee;
>   Draw low and enfold;
> Our souls seek Thee only;
>   O flow, living gold!
>
> Put blindness behind us;
>   O guide us to light;
> Refine us and bind us;
>   O find our hearts right!
>
> Draw low and enfold;
>   O Flame, we invoke Thee;
> O flow, living gold;
>   Our souls seek Thee only!
>
> Our plea is in weakness;
>   O lead us indeed;
> We seek Thee with meekness;
>   O heed our souls' need!

Our souls seek Thee only;
    O flow, living gold;
O Flame, we invoke Thee;
    Draw low and enfold!

Embrace and reclaim us;
    O raise us, we pray;
Sustain and inflame us;
    O blazon our way!

O flow, living gold;
    Our souls seek Thee only;
Draw low and enfold;
    O Flame, we invoke Thee!

L: Now let us raise our consciousness to the legate
level.

Q: How do we raise our consciousness to the legate
level?

L: In general by sending it forth as a living flame,
when we perform the tasks we have selected for our
conscious immortality.

Q: Why should we raise our consciousness to the legate level, at this moment of Sabian assembly?

L: We do so in order that each of us here may be, for
this moment, what all of us should hope to be ultimately.

Q: Many of us have yet to reach the legate level.

L: In the group consciousness we all possess, in the
fullness of its heightening, what any among us may have
achieved along the lines of his own special capacity.

Q: How can we recognize what we have not **ourselves**
achieved?

L: We can recognize the new fullness of our own light within, and in so doing we can clear the self and hold it as a laya center for the total reality here brought to focus.

Q: Will not such an exaltation fade away and be forgotten?

L: Not if we clear the self adequately, by repudiating here and now whatever has brought no welcoming response from some higher value in our daily lives, and in that fashion make this moment an eternal one in our own individual experience.

C: In order that we may recognize the new fullness of our light within, and of the group consciousness in its heightening, let us take encouragement from the message of the Solar Hierarch. And let us pay particular attention to the apportioned strophe in the cycle of our inner sensitiveness.

MESSAGE OF THE HIERARCH

Celebrant

(First lunar month)   The Assurance

Hear now, O seeker who attends me,
  O aspirant, whom I have accepted,
Thus says the Hierarch who established you
  And fashioned you from the beginning
  And will help you;
Fear not, O seeker who attends me,
  My beloved upright one
  Whom I have taken for my own!

(Second lunar month)   The Outpouring

I will pour out the purest potentiality

On those whose sympathies are quickened
And will give of myself without reservation
   To the starved of body and soul;
I will breathe the breath of my eternality
   Into the seed-atoms of your being
And embrace in my eternal consummation
   Your outgivings of inner fire;
Your works shall spring up
   As a fullness of manifestation in plenty,
And be as the shelter of trees
   Along every crowded highway of effort!

(Third lunar month)   *The Dedication*
One worker shall say rather superficially,
   I am a priest of the Brotherhood;
And another may tell all who will listen,
   I am a seeker on the path:
And another may consecrate himself rather ceremoniously
   To the work of the Hierarch
And to gain a title take affiliation
   With some order of illumination.
Thus says the Hierarch, the initiator of aspirants,
   And his superior, the archon of the eternal company,
I am the inception and the completion
   And save through me there is no illumination!

(Fourth lunar month)   *The Witnessing*
Who shall proclaim the glory,
   Says the Hierarch,
And through him
   The archon of the ageless ones.

Publish it and interpret it in my name!
Who else has established the Mysteries
   And announced from of old the events to come;
Let any pretenders reveal what is yet to be!
Know no fear and banish apprehension!
Have I not prepared you
   And explained to you from ancient times?
Are you not my witnesses?
Is there any path to divinity save through me?
I know no other philosopher's stone!

    (Fifth lunar month)   The Great Shame
Those who depend on superficial conceptions
   Are all of them in confusion,
     And the notions in which they delight shall not persist.
They give testimony to outer things
   And have no inner knowledge
     To spare them the shame of their ignorance.
What man has acknowledged a personality as God
   And set up a profitless image for his inspiration?
Behold all his associates shall know shame!
These workers are of men,
   Let them counsel with each other
     And see that there is no divinity within them;
Let them know the terror of their emptiness
   And realize their shame together!

    (Sixth lunar month)   The Adoration of Self
The aspirant on the path of the artisan
   Who seeks development and power within himself
Undergoes discipline to develop his faculties

And subjects his development to the world and passion
And mortifies his spirit with repression of impulse
And builds his God out of his own strength
    By the force of his will for development;
But he is empty within
    And his purpose weakens;
He refuses all normal experience
    And his efforts lose their effectiveness.

(Seventh lunar month)   *The Surrender to the World*
The aspirant on the path of the artist
    Who seeks development in the world
Measures the ideal he would establish
    By the limitation of external conditions.
He accepts the world as he has experienced it;
He adapts his God to the notions he has nurtured;
He reduces his ideal to the circumference
    Of his own self-satisfactions;
He shapes his ideal to the man of transient appetite
    According to the beauty developed in his lusts,
That it may be for worship
    Within the limits of himself.

(Eighth lunar month) The Great Futility
This aspirant goes forth to destroy
    That which does not conform to his conceptions;
He rebuilds into his own ideas
    Some one of the philosophies about him;
He translates his ideas into performance
    That circumstances may strengthen his prejudices;
Then it shall be for him to make himself comfortable

And he takes of his resources
And feels he has every approval for his desires
And he makes a convenience of his conceptions
And claims every reward from the world around him;
Yea, he makes for himself a divine image
And prostrates himself before it
And uses the same materials in self-gratification
And fattens his own vanity;
He makes obeisance to his own conceptions and says,
Illuminate me, for you are my initiator!

(Ninth lunar month) **The Bitter Lesson**
Men know not and do not consider
Since self-centeredness has perverted their vision
And made certain they will not see truth unworthily,
And shrunken their hearts
That they may not know values without experience.
No man calls to mind, or has the understanding to say,
I have taken my God for sensual satisfaction,
I have taken my divine inheritance and debased it.
Shall I make the residue of my effort my God,
Shall I worship what my desire has left unwanted?
Such a one feeds on ashes;
A self-deceived aspiration has turned him aside;
He cannot illuminate his own soul and claim,
There is no delusion in my seeking!

(Tenth lunar month) **The Exhortation**
Remember these things, O seeker,
And you, O aspirant who attends me!
I have fashioned you and you are attending me;

O aspirant, you will not be forgotten by me;
I have isolated your errors of performance
　And swept them away in their superficiality;
I have dissolved your inadequacies
　In their unimportance;
Return to me;
I have freed you from all idle obligation!

　　　(Eleventh lunar month)　*The Indwelling*
Sing O higher planes,
　Sing of the eternal liberation the Hierarch has brought!
Speak the word and give your testimony,
　All you realms of lower manifestation!
Break forth into melody,
　Every peak of self-fulfillment in experience!
Sing O plane of senseborn separations
　And every quickened ego thereon!
The Hierarch has granted initiation
　To the seeker who attends him,
And will incarnate
　In the aspirant who dedicates himself to significance.

　　　(Twelfth lunar month)　*The Fulfillment*
Thus says the Hierarch who frees you from idle obligation
　And has fashioned you from the beginning,
I am the Hierarch
　Who reveals every aspect of manifestation;
Who interprets the cycles of the heavens
　And shows the earth as a fulfillment of its promise,
　Yea, the fulfillment of all things out of themselves;
Who makes as nothing the notions of opportunists

And confounds those who believe they have all answers;
Who asks a proof in works from all who claim great wisdom
And demonstrates the foolishness of idle knowledge.

(Thirteenth lunar month)   *The Eternal Promise*
I am the Hierarch who fulfills the promise
  Of those who speak for me;
Who carries out the works
  Envisioned in my name;
Who says of the invisible fellowship,
  Participation shall be conscious,
And of the centers of illumination within you,
  They shall be brought to the full of their powers,
And of your errors of performance,
  They shall be built more happily into your experience;
Who says to the subconscious and its frustrations,
  Be gone, and I will dry up the roots of your fear;
Who says of the initiate under the Solar Mysteries,
  He shall be my watchman for you;
And who again assures the invisible fellowship,
  It shall be brought to the full of its effectiveness;
And who assures the temple of the Brotherhood,
  Its foundations shall be laid for all who seek the way.

L: In essence then the Solar message, as pertinent to
the present cycle of our lunar sensitiveness, is that we
should

(First month)	Live by every promise of our calling.
(Second month)	Press ahead while many ways are open.
(Third month)	Make our works the proof of our faith.
(Fourth month)	Testify to the wonders we have known.

(Fifth month)   Build on more than superficialities.
(Sixth month)   Know that self alone is powerless.
(Seventh month)   Rise above all shallowness of seeking.
(Eighth month)   Conquer every trace of wilfulness.
(Ninth month)   Guard ourselves from self-deception.
(Tenth month)   Listen for our call to higher service.
(Eleventh month)   Dramatize the magic of our quickening
(Twelfth month)   Realize foundations of eternal scope.
(Thirteenth month) Demonstrate our depth of inspiration.

Q: Are we not challenging ourselves far beyond our strength?

L: Of ourselves our strength is nothing.

C: Our strength is in the Four Manifestations of Solar initiation. These are dramatized in the eternal skies by (1) the pathway through Aries, or the experience of aspiration and the capture of man's heart from the beginning of his pilgrimage, by (2) the pathway through Taurus, or the experience of service and the continual replenishing of self through its own unrestrained expenditure, by (3) the pathway through Gemini, or the experience of fellowship and the endless fulfillment of self in the invisible presence of the Great Ones, and by (4) the pathway through Cancer, or the experience of signatures and the outer sustainment of self in an ever-vital fruition of its efforts.

L: Let us enter the silence of a deep and immortal realization, for three minutes of unvoiced self-inventory and an experience of the power that comes from spiritual self-examination.

Three-minute silence

Celebrant

U: *(Repeating, immediately)*

(First month)

Truly we must live by every promise of our calling.

We thank thee for thy challenge to our faith in thee. We thank thee for thy endless trust in us. We thank thee for the love in which we rest assured.

(Second month)

Truly we must press ahead while all the ways are open.

We thank thee for the wealth of resource at our hand. We thank thee for the chance to spread our works afar. We thank thee for the richness of these days.

(Third month)

Truly we must make our works the tribute to our faith.

We thank thee for protecting us from foolish pride. We thank thee for demanding deeds when words might serve. We thank thee for requiring endlesss sacrifice.

(Fourth month)

Truly we must testify to all the wonders we have known.

We thank thee for the ways of service now revealed. We thank thee for the stress of soul that strengthens us. We thank thee for the chance to prove our worth.

(Fifth month)

Truly we must turn away from superficial values.

We thank thee for the light to see false reasoning. We thank thee for these standards of eternal truth. We thank thee for our growing competence of judgment.

(Sixth month)

Truly we must know that of ourselves we have no power.

We thank thee for the demonstration of thy presence in our work. We thank thee for thy blessing on our aspiration. We thank thee for thy humbling discipline.

(Seventh month)

Truly we must rise above all shallowness of seeking.

We thank thee for protecting us from ways of mere delusion. We thank thee for the eyes to see immortal values. We thank thee for our deepening awareness.

(Eighth month)

Truly we must conquer every trace of wilfulness.

We thank thee for thy scorn when we resort to childish ways. We thank thee for the call to choose the truer course. We thank thee for the sharing of thy wisdom.

(Ninth month)

Truly we must guard ourselves from self-deception.

We thank thee for reviving all our early aspiration. We thank thee for expanding every hope of its achievement. We thank thee for the fresh perspective offered us.

(Tenth month)

Truly we must listen for our call to higher service.

We thank thee for the emphasis on tasks to be performed. We thank thee for directing all attention to the goal. We thank thee for remembering our deeper dedication.

(Eleventh month)

Truly we must dramatize the magic of our quickening.

We thank thee for thy presence as we hasten to our tasks.

We thank thee for removing all distractions on the way.
We thank thee for exalting all our efforts.

(Twelfth month)
Truly we must realize foundations of eternal scope.
We thank thee for the vision that transcends all pride of
     knowledge. We thank thee for the wisdom born of
     self. We thank thee for immortal understanding.

(Thirteenth month)
Truly we must demonstrate our depths of inspiration.
We thank thee for a training that has justified itself. We
     thank thee for the testing that has dramatized our task.
     We thank thee for initiation free of compromise.

A: Now let us raise our consciousness to the acolyte
level.
   Q: How do we raise our consciousness to the acolyte
level?
   A: By endowing our realization of ourselves with a
new significance in the light of our mystery names.
   Q: Many of us have yet to experience the higher self-
ordering of which a mystery name should be the symbol.
   A: In the group consciousness we all rehearse, at any
moment of heightening, what any one among us may be
trying to achieve through his own special capacities.
   Q: Is it for the sake of this rehearsal that we wish to
raise our consciousness to the acolyte level?
   A: Yes, that each for this moment may be the acolyte
of some exalted aspiration represented among us, and
thus experience some one or more facets of his own
higher potential.

Q: How can anyone become the acolyte of any exalted aspiration for just the fleeting half hour of a Full Moon ceremony?

A: By the complete and personal assimilation through the heightened group consciousness of everything from which any enduring worth has been gained by any among us, and by thus strengthening the self as a laya center for the practical values of everyday living.

Q: In what way does this complete and personal but yet vicarious assimilation of these practical values of everyday living make anyone the acolyte of exalted aspiration?

A: By establishing a real foundation for his very literal achievement in the three great necessities and the one great privilege that each worker under the Solar Mysteries must further for all mankind.

STATEMENT OF SABIAN EXPECTATION

Celebrant

We affirm (1) the necessity of health as the means for a maximum self-expression. We acknowledge this physical well-being to be the result of a complete and wholly individual conformity to the root potentials of personal existence. The manifestation of health we identify through an enduring love for all parts of the divine creation. We affirm (2) the necessity of prosperity as a means for a maximum self-consummation. We acknowledge this social well-being to be the result of a complete and wholly individual conformity to the root potentials of society at large. The manifestation of prosperity we identify through a boundless wealth accepted and administered in stewardship for all life. We affirm (3) the necessity of happiness as a means for a maximum self-exaltation. We acknowledge this spiritual well-being to be the result of a complete and wholly individual conformity to the root potentials of the universe itself. The manifestation of happiness we identify through an inner peace or a continuousness of participation in the divine intimacy. We affirm (4) that health, prosperity and happiness are the birthright of every man, and that a spiritual discipline may expect some practical and everyday evidence of physical, social and spiritual well-being in the private and public relationships of every aspirant taking the path to Solar initiation. Moreover we affirm (5) the privilege of understanding as a means for a maximum self-transcendence. We acknowledge this transcendental well-being to be the result of a complete and wholly individual conformity to the creative potentiality of the laya centers and of the control through them of all consciousness at core. The manifestation of understanding we identify as the illimitable and unquenchable hope in which all soul is one.

A: Thus health, prosperity, happiness and understanding become the outer signs of the laya center we each must establish for himself.

Q: Is not the establishment of this far beyond our strength?

A: Of ourselves our strength is nothing.

C: Our strength is in the Four Healings of Solar initiation. These are dramatized in the eternal skies by (1) the pathway through Leo, or the perfection of body that enthrones man as king of the world, by (2) the pathway through Virgo, or the perfection of objective and subjective skills that permits the character of man to develop to its fullest, by (3) the pathway through Libra, or the perfection of personality that facilitates the broadest possible sharing of human experience, and by (4) the pathway through Scorpio, or the perfection of insight that brings the spirit of man to its ultimate unity with the All.

A: Let us enter into the silence of a deep and immortal realization, for two minutes of service as acolytes in behalf of those for whom it is our privilege to ask healing and of experience of the power that comes from spiritual dedication.

Two-minute silence

STATEMENT OF REALIZATION AND THANKS
Celebrant
  U: (Repeating, immediately)

(First month)
Truly we must recognize the nature of our task.
We thank thee for the call to serve thee so completely.
  We thank thee for thy help in overcoming human weakness. We thank thee for the character we build afresh.

(Second month)
Truly we must grasp the opportunity now brought to us.
We thank thee for the service we may render in thy name.
  We thank thee for the plenitude we have to bring to all. We thank thee for the vision we may share.

(Third month)
Truly we must bring ourselves to deeper realization.
We thank thee for rejecting all our empty claims. We
thank thee for inspiring us through every depth of
self. We thank thee for directing us to worthy ends.

(Fourth month)
Truly we must strive to merit our acceptance.
We thank thee for the privilege of living our own promise.
We thank thee for encouragement at every point of
need. We thank thee for our days of endless growth.

(Fifth month)
Truly we must search our souls for worthless notions.
We thank thee for the shame that checks our foolishness.
We thank thee for thy patience when we falter on the
way. We thank thee for thy presence in our hearts.

(Sixth month)
Truly we must shape our lives more worthily.
We thank thee for the chance to plumb to greater depth
of self. We thank thee for rejecting all our senseless
claims. We thank thee for the resolution of our pride.

(Seventh month)
Truly we must meet the world in more creative fashion.
We thank thee for the insights of a better way. We thank
thee for the urge to break our bonds of blindness. We
thank thee for thy answer to our every aspiration.

(Eighth month)
Truly we must face ourselves with very deep concern.
We thank thee for the chance to stop all waste of self

We thank thee for thy light in every darkness of our making. We thank thee for thy presence at our hand.

(Ninth month)

Truly we must understand the burden we should share.
We thank thee for reminding us of duties long neglected.
We thank thee for revealing this distortion of our faith.
We thank thee for our new horizons now.

(Tenth month)

Truly we must quicken every loyal instinct of our being.
We thank thee for appealing to our inner sense of right.
We thank thee for reminding us that we have pledged ourselves. We thank thee for reordering our vision.

(Eleventh month)

Truly we must prove our readiness for service.
We thank thee for discouraging all lesser enterprise. We thank thee for sustaining true perspective. We thank thee for assuring us of thy descent within our hearts.

(Twelfth month)

Truly we must realize our source in true beginnings.
We thank thee for thy lessons in reliance from within. We thank thee for our freedom from all transient fads of faith. We thank thee for experience at core.

(Thirteenth month)

Truly we must pour our lives into eternal service.
We thank thee for the depths of search demanded of us. We thank thee for the rigors of the seeking. We thank thee for revealing all the greater work ahead.

N: Now let us raise our consciousness to the neophyte level.

Q: How do we raise our consciousness to the neophyte level?

N: By channeling it anew in the aspiration that first led each of us to dedicate himself to service under the Solar Mysteries.

Q: Why should we raise our consciousness to the neophyte level?

N: That each of us may know for a moment the full magic of the philosopher's stone that he has been asked to refine for himself.

Q: How can we know we actually are refining a philosopher's stone in our own personal lives?

N: By our increasing disinterest in things that are of no value, and our continuing eagerness to center the self within itself as a laya center for the invisible fellowship.

Q: Can each different seeker create a laya center for the invisible fellowship as a whole?

N: It is that very individuality of it that constitutes it the philosopher's stone, and gives it the power to touch all things in a unifying magic.

Q: But if this personal laya center is born of its own individual aspiration, is it not caught up in all the limitations and narrowed perspective of the separated personality?

N: Foundations are foundations, however necessary a deepening and a broadening may be from time to time, and we facilitate a Solar initiation as we give the least of personality our full respect and indeed acknowledge the fundamental integrity of everything that exists.

STATEMENT OF SABIAN OBJECTIVE

Celebrant

Our objective is the restoration of the Solar Mysteries. By Solar we signify the proving from within, and by Mysteries the Eternal Wisdom, and in making our statement of objective we show forth our acceptance of the integrity of man and of his world respectively. The proving from within demands an uncompromising respect for personality, or for each person's right to determine his own self-justification, and in consequence we avoid all gratuitous distinctions among people as well as all public recognition of spiritual merit. The Eternal Wisdom represents an absolute philosophy, and by absolute we do not mean that everything is referred to some supposed unchanging primary but rather that the totality of existence is brought to order in a complete series of graduated and comprehensible steps. These we recognize as stages in an unceasing division of labor. Thus man's most exalted concepts are linked at every point with the knowledge he gains in the course of his everyday affairs, and all enduring insights come to center ultimately in that individual realization through which they can be verified and shared. The Solar Mysteries are restored as the whole span of history on the one hand, and the illimitable spread of human experience on the other, are brought to conscious focus in an effective here and now.

N: As we prove everything from within, and pay every due to the practical world in which we find ourselves, we develop the wisdom that brings all being into an immortal unity of our own creation.

Q: Is this not a responsibility far beyond our strength?

N: Of ourselves our strength is nothing.

C: Our strength is in the Four Landmarks of Solar initiation. These are dramatized in the eternal skies by (1) the pathway through Sagittarius, or the respect for personality that should characterize all our contact with our fellows:

N: Now let us stand, and shake hands to the right and to the left in simple fellowship of the spirit.

Ritual of the hand clasp

C: By (2) the pathway through Capricorn, or the respect for the community and nation that should characterize our fellowship in every performance of our civic duties:

N: Now let us, with a right hand on the heart and facing towards the capital of the country in which we hold citizenship, silently affirm our allegiance to the immortal values in human society.

Ritual of civic loyalty

C: By (3) the pathway through Aquarius, or the respect for the group consciousness that should characterize all our allegiances and activities in the fellowship of the Solar Mysteries:

N: Now let each of us in turn inscribe his name in the archives of the Solar Mysteries, as this heightened moment of spiritual rehearsal provides an agency for the total re-commital to the eternal vision.

Ritual of inscription

C: And by (4) the pathway through Pisces, or the respect for the invisible and immortal fellowship in which we strive to live and move and have our being.

N: Now let us clasp our hands behind our backs, in token of our fidelity to everything everywhere that ever has contributed to our own ongoing and that in this moment and always may help us forward and upward.

C: What is your report on your faithfulness?

U: All is well.

N: Now let us be seated and enter into the silence of a deep and immortal realization, for one minute of an unvoiced direction of self and an experience that comes from spiritual perspective.

One-minute silence

STATEMENT OF REALIZATION AND THANKS
Celebrant
U: (*Repeating, immediately*)

(*First month*)
Truly we must dedicate our lives to deeper purpose.
We thank thee for reminding us of things that we can do.
We thank thee for assuring us of thy sustaining help.
We thank thee for removing all our fears.

(*Second month*)
Truly we must quicken to the needs of those about us.
We thank thee for revealing what the higher life may be.
We thank thee for accepting us as seekers on the path.

We thank thee for demanding this totality of giving.

(Third month)
Truly we must look beyond the empty show of life.
We thank thee for the more enduring goals revealed to us. We thank thee for thy guidance as we dedicate ourselves. We thank thee for the quickening we gain.

(Fourth month)
Truly we must quicken to a soul-reviving fervor.
We thank thee for demanding deeper purpose in our effort. We thank thee for reminding us that we must live for others. We thank thee for expanding our ideals.

(Fifth month)
Truly we must learn to recognize the higher path.
We thank thee for requiring a worthiness of goal. We thank thee for disclosing sham and mere pretension. We thank thee for directing us to truth in every facet.

(Sixth month)
Truly we must gain perspective in our quest.
We thank thee for reordering our efforts on the path. We thank thee for denying our pretense to special fitness. We thank thee for encouraging our self-examination.

(Seventh month)
Truly we must find real channels for our seeking.
We thank thee for rebuking our acceptance of vain notions. We thank thee for thy warning when we tend to go astray. We thank thee for thy insight in our effort.

(Eighth month)
Truly we must ask for guidance in our overeager seeking.

We thank thee for thy patience in our rush to reach the goal. We thank thee for thy vision of an endless poise. We thank thee for thy revelation of the better path.

(Ninth month)

Truly we must see how superficial we have been.

We thank thee for revealing all the madness of our course. We thank thee for persuading us to change our ways. We thank thee for restoring worthy points of view.

(Tenth month)

Truly we must recognize our deeper obligations.

We thank thee for encouraging a greater self-enlistment. We thank thee for demanding that we put ourselves to work. We thank thee for revealing talents long unused.

(Eleventh month)

Truly we must understand the imminent indwelling.

We thank thee for the drama of eternal incarnation. We thank thee for our part to play in its performance. We thank thee for the living magic of its message.

(Twelfth month)

Truly we must learn to hold to all our reassurance.

We thank thee for protecting us from passing foolishness. We thank thee for thy discipline in thinking clearly. We thank thee for these insights of eternal life.

(Thirteenth month)

Truly we must show appreciation of our high estate.

We thank thee for rejecting all our lesser gifts of self. We thank thee for our lessons in discrimination. We thank thee for accepting our sincerity at root.

Chaldean Dismissal

Celebrant

We charge the solvent of Saturn
  With the deepening of your understanding;
To Jupiter we entrust the giving-forth
  That permits your inner growth;
In Mars we place a trust
  To keep you active in the world;
From Venus we demand for you
  The essence of experience;
And of Mercury we command a revelation
  Through the word that admits to the Brotherhood!

QUARTERLY MEETING

CHALLENGE OF THE HIERARCH

Leader

The Solar Hierarch stands within
  The temple of the Brotherhood;
He grants assignments to the Masters.

How much longer dwell ye in externals
  And tolerate the pretensions of the idle?

Hasten to those despoiled of their heritage;
Hasten to those cast off from above;
Rescue those enslaved to illusion;
Nourish those who starve within;
  Awaken the sleeping ones;
  Assure the starving ones;
Take these from the ministry of spinners of words!

The masses know not, and will not understand,
  But drift along in darkness;
The mighty on the earth are concerned with trifles!

I have said, ye are priests
  And all of you offspring of the Word;
Why die ye like men
  For gain of princely trappings?

Arise, O inner flame, and go forth
  To ensoul the nations!

Ceremonies of recognition

WELCOMING ADDRESS
(For new students on July 3d and December 31st)

Leader

By simple virtue of the fact that you are seeking illumination, full illumination shall be yours. You have, by taking the first step, committed yourself irrevocably to the journey. And to begin the journey assures you that you will arrive at the goal, as inevitably as anything that is impelled by spirit and so is subject no longer to the lesser necessities of a purely transient reality. Difficulties may encompass you, but you will surmount them. Delays may hinder you, but time will dissolve into nothingness. Other calls on you and all the pressing demands of outer and material life may seem to interrupt your progresss, but such interruptions will be so only in the realm of seeming. From now and henceforth you are destined to press on in the daytime and by night, consciously and unconsciously, in summer and in winter, and never for one moment turning aside from your progress to the end. You have wished to become an initiate, and an accepted candidate you are now and from the first moment of your conception of initiation. And in the realm of potentials you truly are illuminated already. Day by day your consciousnesss will expand, for initiation is nothing else but an expansion of consciousness, and though for a long time to come you yourself may not recognize your status it yet exists. You are superman now, and in seeking less than the greatest of goals you are untrue to yourself. So think magnificently, for in the realm of thought your destiny is established, and talk modestly, for in the realm of men your temptations arise. In the enduring things of reality you will be more and more alone, since your sustenance and strengthening in matters of eternity are not to be defined or made known in conceptions of this world. But in your aloneness you will find the greater companionship of those who are stimulating without exactions, or of those who are too filled with divinity to have room for petty considerations. Prepare to take your place with the immortals. Hail, initiate of tomorrow!

Discourse on Achievement
(For acolytes and legates, Palm Sunday and October 17th)
Leader

Now that you have stood consciously within the Temple of the Mysteries, you have gained for yourself an office in the world. At this stage of your growth you have been sent back into the realm of everyday, there to translate appreciation into experience and desire into achievement. You have become a personage! Authority that is certified by the golden seal of the Illuminated Ones now placed on your heart, and always to be seen by the inward vision in quiet hours of meditation, may be demonstrated by you at will in the presence of men and through every vortex of affairs. Your voice has been given a spiritual resonance that will resound to all ears, if you will give it utterance. The world however will make but empty response to any claims you may make of divine authority, for the reason that there is nothing spiritual in word alone, and if you yield to the temptation to speak aloud of these experiences of the spirit you will only destroy the realities of the Temple in your consciousness. Then the Mysteries may fade away within your memory, and you may find yourself again beyond the outer portal and under necessity to start once more from the beginning. Therefore you are not sent into the world to make the idle claims of those who have no surety within themselves, but are returned for a season in order that you may stamp your name on the tablets of time. At this stage in your growth your spiritual identity is as yet withheld from you, for the reason that you still must discharge your steward-ship of the physical heritage entrusted to you through your flesh-and-blood parents. As you bring credit to this outer citizenship, you will be qualified to bring glory to the ultimate mystery name to be found only in the Book of Aspiration. Because you have passed beyond the pos-sibility of more than temporary failure in your spiritual being, you will continue to be a member of the Assembly, but your spiritual stature is yet to be determined. You may stand as tall or short as you wish, since this stature is established entirely by deeds in the world. Hail initiate of today!

Inspirational program

DISCOURSE ON INSPIRATION
(For July 3d and December 31st)

Leader

Because you have entered the Temple of the Mysteries, you stand now in the presence of a mighty company. No matter how small or how large your part in these spiritual things may be, you have at this moment been given the right hand of fellowship. The interior of this Temple may be dark to your eyes, and to your ears there may be neither sound nor stir of life, but it is possible for you to see and to hear and to awaken all your senses in their higher functioning. This is a simple expansion of consciousness that shortly will be yours. For an awakening to a realization of the friendly assembly of workers who surround you, and bathe you in the effulgence of a light you do not see and greet you with words you cannot hear, it is only necessary that you enter into the laya center that has cradled this company. As you have of your own volition crossed the threshold of the Temple, so may you by your own desire both see and hear. This is a mighty company because it is established through no relationship of personality, and through no desire for personal power. Here are those who have caught the challenge of the new heaven and earth. They are the quiet and silent workers who have held the needs and problems of humanity in consciousness for many thousands of years. Here is a fellowship of high initiates, and its ranks are made up in the largest part by those who have served life after life. Who knows but that you may have been a member of this group in the past, and require only the first flash of enlightenment to restore you to your exalted status? But if this be your first hesitant step toward illumination, you are equally welcome. Binding these souls together is the challenge of a work to be done. For the opening of your eyes and your ears it is necessary that you participate in this challenge. Is there not something you can see to do? Is your world of everyday any better for your living? Do your friends flourish because of your near presence? Does everyone everywhere smile and feel lighter of heart when you pass by? Remember that the gaining of inspiration can result only from the giving of inspiration. Hail, inspired one!

DISCOURSE ON STEWARDSHIP
(For Palm Sunday and October 17th)

Leader

You have returned to the world and now you have found, in the light of the higher understanding developed within you, that the world is far from the narrow and bitter place you had thought it to be. You have learned the great truth that the Temple of the Mysteries is situated in the domain of everyday, and is concealed only from the idly curious and the coldly self-seeking. You have stood within the Temple consciously, and there you have been welcomed into the presence of the mighty company of immortal ones. And at last you have realized that this journey has been wholly a matter of consciousness. You stand as you always have stood, in the world of men, but you are transformed. No longer does the dull and utterly drab aspect of life face you, since your eyes have achieved a new dimension of appreciation and your heart has expanded in a new range of sympathy. Your steps may take you down the same streets in the shadow of the same buildings, and past the same faces and their evidence of the blind and often hopeless rush of human kind. But now the streets are Mystery Streets. They are lined with spiritual gold, and decorated with the precious stones of inner understanding. The sound of confusion in your ears has become the cosmic melody of eternal spheres. The closeness of humanity conjures up in your nostrils the alluring perfume of a very essence of fellowship. Children of God are these, all of them, and if they be hard or unwashed it is because no greater soul has bent to lead them to the light. Into your heart wells the incorruptible understanding of the Elder Brothers, with whom your lot now is cast, and everywhere you find yourself the steward of eternal values. You discover that illness is no longer yours, except as you may accept the disruptive substance of inharmony for its transmutation. Poverty is no longer yours, whether of soul or material things, for you are custodian of illimitable wealth and you dwell as a Prince of Spirit should. Unhappiness you will never know again, since forever now your pain is joy. Hail, ambassador of the hierarchies!

Testimony and discussion period

PRAYER TO THE FULLNESS OF THE YEAR

Leader

For our lack of gratitude we beg Thy indulgence,
  Giver of Richest Gifts!
For our lack of accomplishment we ask Thy forgetfulness,
  O Source of Sustainment Everlasting!
For our lack of inner faith we entreat Thy understanding,
  Sublime Revelation of Power!
And for our willingness to try again and again
  We seek Thy blessing, Father of All in All!

ACOLYTE MEETING

MEDITATION ON THE SOLAR BREATH

Leader

Thou, Solar Breath, we recognize;
We seek to aid all life to flow;
    O Breath, let us achieve with Thee!
Indwell in all our enterprise;
Forgive us when we see but woe;
    O Breath, we wish to flow with Thee!

Thou, Solar Breath, we energize;
We seek to aid all kind to grow;
    O Breath, let us expand with Thee!
Be Thou the strength we realize;
Forgive us for all fear we show;
    O Breath, we wish to grow with Thee!

Thou, Solar Breath, we idolize;
We seek to aid all light to glow;
    O Breath, let us shine forth with Thee!
Be Thou what we immortalize;
Forgive us when our hearts are low;
    O Breath, we wish to glow with Thee!

Thou, Solar Breath, we solemnize;
We seek to aid all minds to know;
    O Breath, let us reach up with Thee!

Be with us in our least surmise;
Forgive us when our thoughts are slow;
O Breath, we wish to know with Thee!

Admission of tardy members

Ritual of candle lighting

Acolyte exposition and discussion

ACOLYTE DISMISSAL

Leader
From our communion with the inner self
  May we take forth real outer fruits!
We dedicate ourselves anew to our own flesh and blood,
  That all our loved ones may have strength in us;
We dedicate ourselves anew to our own broader heritage,
  That we may bless all others of our land and race;
And we dedicate ourselves anew to all the world,
  That we may help create a universal fellowship!

MESSAGE OF EZEKIEL

The Calling of Ezekiel
I attained ordination by the Brotherhood
  At the close of thirty years
  On the fourth plane of being
  And in the fifth evolution of self-consciousness.
Then I became aware of my initiations
  And I gained perspective of the cosmic scheme.
This fifth evolution of self-consciousness
  Corresponded to the fifth initiation.
The power of the hierarchies
  Was definitely strengthened in me,
  Who had been born to my task.
I took cognizance of my commission
  Among the custodians of the Mysteries,
And among those who possessed arcane knowledge
  I became spokesman for the Great Central Flame.
I applied my insight to understanding.
The Master Thesis of Ezekiel
And behold, a solar system was born
  Emanating as a breath of God;
A great forming mass of cosmic substance
  In which spirit caught and clothed itself.
Out of the midst thereof came a brightness:
  The golden fire of God!
And there were four elements

And four natures and four spheres
From which sprang the likeness of living creatures;
Four and four and four, or a man!
His feet were plunged into the star dust of matter;
His hands within the spheres groped for being.
The natures were the triplicities:
The water-carrier and the lion,
Air and fire in the realm of spirit;
And the ox and scorpion,
Earth and water beneath;
Whipped into nebulous shapes with the birth of planets.
Thus were the natures
While the spheres were divided above
Co-operating one with the other but not changing,
Enmeshing spirit in the quadrature of experience.
The lamp of the spirit like a coal of fire
Moved upward and downward within the man,
And out of the fire flashed lightning!
The four, four and four formed a wheel
That lay on the earth and defined the man,
And the elements were a wheel
And the natures a wheel within the wheel.
There were men
And when they moved the wheel moved but turned not.
Wheresoever the spirit went
There was the wheel lifted up;
For the understanding and life of the spirit
Dwelt within the wheel.
Above stretched the firmament, a crystal
Where the spheres thundered the voice of the Almighty.
In the heavens lay the cosmic man;

The covenant of the zodiac
With fire flashing from Libra upward and downward:
The glory of the Lord!
The Calling of Ezekiel (Continued)
When I realized the nature of the arcane knowledge
  I had drawn to understanding
  I was humble.
And I heard the voice of authority commanding me.
The Commission of Ezekiel
And this voice said to me,
  Initiate, be conscious in thy higher vehicles
  And I will express myself through thee!
Whereupon divine consciousnesss dwelt within me
  And I heard the voice that spoke through me.
Initiate, I send thee to all whom I have called,
  To a group that is self-sufficient
  And that has drawn away from me.
They and their leaders have perverted my teachings
  Even to this day.
And their works are arrogant
  And without divine compassion,
And I will send thee to them and thou shall say to them,
  Thus command the creative hierarchies!
Whether or not they will accept thee
  Or draw away in their self-sufficiency,
They yet shall know
  There has been a divine voice among them!
And thou, initiate, admit no power in them,
  Neither admit potency to their claims.
Though they tangle and taunt and sting thee,
  Fear not their words,

Nor be discouraged by the virtue of their works,
　　For they are a self-sufficient group.
Thou, initiate, listen always to my voice within,
　　Neither be self-sufficient
　　　As the arrogant ones who claim me.
Rather open thy being;
　　Draw into thyself that which I give thee.
I applied my insight to understanding,
　　And the Great Central Flame was manifest within me
　　And all the knowledge of the Mysteries
　　Opened up before me,
　　Revealed outwardly and inwardly at once,
And with knowledge was severance of the past
　　And expiation and bitter inner experience.
The voice of authority said to me,
　　Initiate, draw into thyself
　　That which rests now in thy understanding,
　　And go teach all whom I have called.
So I opened my being
　　And by divine command drew all into myself,
　　And the voice said,
Initiate, quicken thy aspiration
　　And fill thy external being with this consciousness,
And I filled myself and divine understanding
　　Was sweet in my being with the satisfaction of service.
Then the voice of authority said to me,
　　Initiate, go dwell among those I have called,
　　And interpret thy conceptions of me to them.
For I do not send thee to a people
　　Immersed in sensual experience
　　Or with no knowledge of the divine,

But to those whom I have called.
Not to the broad sweep of humanity,
  Sensual and unstudied in truth,
  Whose passions would seem strange to thee;
Surely if I sent thee to them they would learn of thee!
But those I have called will not listen to thee
  As they will not respond to my voice within;
  For all I have called are stubborn of intellect
  And have stifled their aspirations and sympathies.
Behold, I have made thy pretensions
  Arrogant against their pretensions,
  And thy intellect coldly efficient
  Against their intelligence.
As a crystallization harder than diamond
  Have I made thy understanding!
Fear not nor be upset at their arrogance,
  For they are a self-sufficient group.
Moreover the voice of authority said to me,
  Initiate, all my conceptions that I evolve in thee,
  Receive in thy inner compassion
  And acknowledge with thy senses.
And go, get thee to those tangled in truth,
  Even those trained by the ones I have chosen,
  And say,
  Thus command the creative hierarchies!
  Whether they accept this or abide in their own ideas.
                The Ordination of Ezekiel
Then I became ecstatic and heard
  As though supporting me
  The music of the spheres in motion,
  Sounding the glory of the hierarch of the solar system.

The spheres of all sentient life I saw
  Co-operating one with the other,
  And the manifestation of the great wheel of the zodiac
  Distributing cosmic fire.
Therefore I was ecstatic and raised up in understanding,
  And I entered on my work sharp to impression,
And with the driving urge of illumination,
  Spokesman for the Great Central Flame.
I came to those tangled in truth,
  Isolated by a measure of understanding;
  To those who sought the Solar initiation;
  And I accepted the karmic limitation for seven ordeals.
I attained priesthood at the end of the seventh initiation.
The power of the hierarchs was strengthened within me.
The hierarch said, initiate, I have made thee
  Watchman over those I have chosen;
  Therefore understand the expression of my being
  And give them warning from me.
When I say to the idlers,
  They shall surely become industrious,
  And thou do not transmit the understanding
  Nor teach to warn the idler from his fruitless way,
The idle individual shall engender karma
  As a laggard in evolution
  And the conscious guidance of his higher self
  I shall require of thee at another time.
Yet if thou attempt to give understanding
  And the idler persist in useless living,
  He shall continue incarnation as a laggard
  And thou will have delivered thy obligation as priest.
Again, when an active worker turns from his work

And becomes enmeshed in useless byways
And fails in some test established by the hierarchies
Because thou did not give him understanding,
He shall incarnate as a laggard
And his good works shall be lost for want of growth
While the conscious guidance of his higher self
I shall require eventually of thee.
Nevertheless if thou teach understanding
Of the continuity of effort,
So that the active worker does not deviate,
He shall continue in consciousness through understanding,
And thou will have delivered thy obligation as priest.

The Ministry of Ezekiel

I became spokesman for the Great Central Flame
And the hierarch commanded me,
Assert thyself! Go forth into the ordinary walks of life
And there I will use thee.
Then I asserted myself and went forth
Into the ordinary walks of life,
And behold the manifestation of the hierarchies was clear,
Even the manifestation I had known in my own being,
And I was humble.
Then I became ecstatic and confident
And I heard the voice of authority commanding me,
Go, shut thyself in thy house,
For behold, initiate, they shall flatter thee,
And win thee with cajolery,
But thou shall not be led into public work.
I will give thee control of thy speech
So that thou shall not speak at all
To feed their own conceptions,

For they are a self-sufficient group.
But when I manifest in thee I shall inspire thy speech,
    And thou shall say to them, Thus say the hierarchies!
He that understands, let him understand,
    And he that draws away, let him draw away,
    For they are a self-sufficient group.

THE SABIAN PLEDGES

The Neophyte Pledge

(A) Affirming that my supreme desire is the achievement of divine illumination, and that the purpose in such desire is to earn a definite commission of stewardship as a conscious participant in the Eternal Wisdom;

(B) Realizing that individual commissions under the Solar Mysteries must be self-bestowed, and that authority of this nature can result only from some self-assumed obligation that will commit my spiritual self by an objectification of this desire;

(C) Understanding that the higher consciousness of the individual corresponds by spiritual dimension with the normal consciousness of the group, and that the power that identity of purpose creates in a group is made available for the committing of my higher self through my activity within such a group;

(D) Determining that my entire being shall be united by binding all my lower and higher principles to this one purpose, and that the desire of my lower will for my higher self shall now gain objectivity through the group consciousness inherent in this pledge;

(1) I hereby declare that the desire for expanded consciousness that brings me before the Sabian Portal of the Solar Mysteries shall be kept the actuating influence in all my lesser desires through the whole of my life, as far

as I can achieve control of my being, and I recognize this pledge as in no way dependent on present or future associations with any teaching, organization or person.

(2) Moreover, as an earnest of my serious intent, I promise that for two years from this date I will attend a study group of the Sabian Assembly each week, or make a written report on my thoughts and endeavors in connection with my Sabian committal for each week in which I do not attend such a group, and that for the period of my participation in the activities of the Assembly I will contribute regularly to its support.

The Acolyte Pledge

(A) Affirming that as fruitage of my two years or more of self-assumed discipline I have achieved an enlargement of consciousness I can identify definitely to myself, and that I desire to advance to a point of further spiritual development;

(B) Realizing that individual commissions of stewardship under the Solar Mysteries must be self-bestowed, and that authority of this nature can result only from some regularly performed duty in connection with group consciousness;

(C) Understanding that the acolyte grade of self-commitment marks a willingness on my part to meet the world on the basis of its everyday standards of excellence, and at the same time and without ever drawing attention to myself in connection therewith to accept new responsibilities in the invisible fellowship of which I am a part and to give these constant precedence in my underlying interest;

(D)   Determining to link my past and my future or my experiences and my potentialities in a present service to the world, and to develop my persistence of personality to the point of a complete and constant use of the entire heritage of my prior being;

(1)   I hereby declare that the conviction of conscious immortality that has been objectified by my passing through the Sabian Portal of the Solar Mysteries shall be kept the determining factor in every enlargement of my consciousness through the entire continuance of my personality, as far as I may be able to influence my incarnations in the present life stream of human expresssion, and I recognize this pledge as in no way dependent on present or future associations with any teaching, organization, person or invisible intelligence.

(2)   Moreover, as an earnest of my serious intent, I promise that following my enlistment as an acolyte I will attend sixty-three consecutive Full Moon meetings of the Sabian Assembly either in person or by proxy, and that for the period of my participation in this discipline I will serve as a worker in consciousness for the Assembly and will continue to contribute regularly to its support.

The Legate Pledge

(A)   Affirming that as a result of my seven years or more of self-assumed discipline I have created a laya center in the conscious administration of the spiritual destiny of my race and generation, such as has been identified to me in objective fashion, and that I desire to establish this personal nucleation as an eternal commission of self;

(B)   Realizing that individual commissions of stewardship under the Solar Mysteries must be self-bestowed, and that authority of this nature can result only from some permanent association with the group consciousness of those already so commissioned;

(C) Understanding that the legate grade of self-commitment marks a necessity on my part to serve the world in its everyday affairs and to gain a recognition for my ambassadorship of the Solar Mysteries by excellencies that will be judged as such by this outer world, and that I must prove my spiritual development by demonstrating it through a wholly objective normality;

(D) Determining to assimilate my personality to the world soul in such fashion that my major persistence of being shall be in the hearts of men, and to serve myself through this larger selfhood alone;

(1) I hereby declare that the conviction of conscious fellowship with the Great Ones of the ages as this has been objectified for me in the course of the Sabian discipline shall actuate me in a conscious continuance of my stewardship through every aspect of my influence in the world of everyday, as far as I may be able to create a contribution to the world that the world of itself will seek to maintain, and I recognize this pledge as in no way dependent on present or future associations with any teaching, organization, person, invisible intelligence or aspect of deity.

(2) Moreover, as an earnest of my serious intent, I promise that I will spend an hour in strictest solitude preceding my attendance at each of twelve consecutive quarterly meetings of the Sabian Assembly, and that for the period of my participation in the legate or any higher

discipline I will serve on a consciousness quadrangle and continue to contribute regularly to the support of the Assembly.

THE JUNIOR PLEDGE

(A) I desire to have an active part in the activities of the Sabian Assembly.

(B) My motive is (a) that I may have the inspiration that comes from associating with people who have dedicated their lives to more than gratifying their appetites and pursuing their selfish interests, (b) that with the help of spiritual precept and example I may develop my own character to the point where I am worthy of association with all the dedicated men and women I may come to know and (c) that through faithfulness to the common objectives uniting those who seek the Sabian way to greater understanding in special self-dedication I may gain some great vision of my own and be able to dedicate my own life to its fulfillment.

(1) Therefore I promise to perform some specific and tangible service in connection with the Sabian procedures as this may (a) be convenient for the members of the Assembly and (b) prove rewarding to me in performing it.

(2) I am not yet fifteen years of age, and this enlistment for Sabian service has the approval of my parents or guardians.

THE SABIAN LESSONS AND IMPRIMATUR

801-848   The Mosaic Prophecy   (96)   E
  Series 33   March 30, 1931; October 20, 1947
849-874   Symbolical Astrology   (54)   C
  Series 34   May 18, 1931
875-900   Plato's Atlantis   (53)   D
  Series 35   October 12, 1931; October 15, 1951
901-925   Theosophical Astrology   (51)   E
  Series 36   November 16, 1931
926-949   Pauline Theology   (48)   G
  Series 37   February 29, 1932; January 25, 1954
950-976   Modern Thought   (55)   K
  Series 38   April 11, 1932; April 10, 1961
977-1000   Directional Astrology   (49)   L
  Series 39   May 9, 1932
1001-1024   Pauline Eschatology   (48)   G
  Series 40   August 15, 1932; July 12, 1954
1025-1050   Plato's Banquet   (53)   M
  Series 41   October 17, 1932; October 12, 1953
1051-1076   Arabian Astrology   (53)   L
  Series 42   October 24, 1932
1077-1100   Pauline Mysticism   (48)   G
  Series 43   January 30, 1933; December 27, 1954
1101-1126   Sabian Fundamentals   (53)   A
  Series 44   April 17, 1933
1127-1150   Hermetic Astrology   (49)   E
  Series 45   April 24, 1933
1151-1174   Pauline Authority   (48)   G
  Series 46   July 17, 1933; June 13, 1955
1175-1200   Hegelian Astrology   (53)   M
  Series 47   October 9, 1933

Notes

Lessons 1-45 were not prepared in written form. The outlines for the initial presentations are mimeographed and available as *The Occult Principles*. Lessons 31-38 were developed as the book *Key Truths of Occult Philosophy,* now out of print but with its text mimeographed and available as one of the Sabian library sets. Lessons 39-45, originally outlines for a proposed book *Key Principles of Astrology*, were subsequently redeveloped in series 26 as *Temple Astrology*. Lessons 114-175, from June 3, 1925, through August 5, 1926, presented continuing lessons in *The Codex Occultus* on alternate weeks with *Modern Philosophy* and *The Secret Doctrine*, and in consequence a skip sequence of lesson numbering will be found in these three series. The studies in *Grimm's Fairy Tales* were interrupted and then resumed on August 12, 1926.

Extra lessons needed in order to include four of the sets in the regular philosophy-symbolism cycle are 3001-3002, added to *Studies in Alice* in October, 1955; 3003-3004, required by the *Art of Wisdom* in September-October, 1965; 3005-3011, required by *Grimm's Fairy Tales* in September-October, 1966; and 3012-3015 required by *The Secret Doctrine* in October, 1967.

The regular cycle for the Bible lessons is established in the 1945-65 reissue, and the third reissue of the Biblical studies in the same order begins with *The Promised Land* on February 8, 1965.

The regular cycle for the philosophy-symbolism lessons is not established until after the third reissue of the various series, since a longer period of adjustment has seemed wise in achieving a full spread of the studies in Plato, Plotinus and Aristotle. These were presented originally through a concentrated attention to each in 1929-34, 1934-40 and 1940-5 respectively, but this arrangement gives too specialized a character to different phases of the cycle. Conversely, however, keeping several other groups of related studies in relatively close sequence has proved helpful as an aid to general balance in the approach to the Eternal Wisdom. The third cycle begins with *Plato's Republic* on October 11, 1965. *Grimm's Fairy Tales* is added to the cycle at that time, starting on April 11, 1966. In the fourth cycle, and as necessary in subsequent cycles to keep a starting philosophy lesson on or near October 17th, its twenty-seventh lesson will be omitted. *Ibn Gabirol's Source of Life* starts in the third cycle on October 17, 1966, and with the fourth cycle and thereafter this fundamental series in Sabian insights will be the beginning point in assigning philosophy-symbolism lessons to their dates. Following the Ibn Gabirol studies in 1966 *The Secret Doctrine* is added to the cycle, starting on April 17, 1967. In the third cycle *Plato's Banquet* and *Plotinian Destiny* exchange position. At the threshold of the fourth cycle *Aristotle's Taxonomy* and *Plato's Republic* exchange position.

Virtually all lesson series are used ultimately in the philosophy-symbolism and Bible cycles on the one hand, or on the other are included in the twenty-four issued in an individual sequence to each student in the astrology discipline and the five supplied to acolytes similarly. *Conceptual Training* and *Modern Philosophy* are superceded by more detailed expositions of Plotinus and academic philosophy, respectively. *Sabian Fundamentals* is given to each newcomer as he makes his affiliation with the Assembly. *Chaldean Initiation* and the *Codex Occultus* are specialized subject matter, but are available for supplementing the other studies.

INDEX OF RITUALS AND IMPRIMATUR

The Pledges, their Imprimatur and Index

APPENDIX
THE 1976 ADJUSTMENT

When with January 1st of this new year a more satisfactory distribution was arranged for the author's hard-
cover books, the result was an immediate selling off of the
basic stock of the *Sabian Manual*. An ultimate rewriting of
this manual, originally issued for his students only, has
long been necessary in view of the changing conditions of
human society in general. To do so now however would
not be too advantageous, with global transitions so very
uncertain at this point. Currently the book has had supplementary mimeographed instructions for members of the
Sabian Assembly, but that has not proved too satisfactory
and something better should be provided. Complicating
matters is considerable indication that in its present activities the Sabian Assembly may gradually swing back to the
group-meeting pattern from the present student-afield one,
or to what was its original form of discipline, still prevailing
when the *Manual* was published in 1957. Any appreciable
editing at this fluid moment in history might not hold as
perhaps it should to the initial formulations actually first
put together in the earlier *Ritual of Living* in 1930. That,
as coincident with the discovery of the planet Pluto and
probable first stirrings of the new great or Aquarian Age of
mankind, suggests caution now in any too specific estima-
tion of future trends.

In consequence it seems wise to reprint with only the

slightest changes in the existing text but adding in, as an appendix, what points of interpretation or added explanation might well be stressed as needed help in understanding the *Manual* while the global shifts are so exceptionally significant in everyday living.

With the years there has been an increasing demand for information on the part of those more interested in learning something about the Sabian project than in gaining any detailed mastery of its procedures and materials. The *Manual* therefore, in the course of the explanation it provides, should meet the need for such an essentially classificatory description of itself. In other words, it should identify its proper place in the history of human thought. As perhaps being more than anything else a presentation and demonstration of a way of thinking, its possible contribution to man's intellectual developments is as an independent or free philosophy in distinction from (1) a religion or an association of the sort that above all else demands a blind faith in itself together with a strict obedience to the authority it may be able to establish for itself, or (2) an educational group making an equivalent demand of total acceptance by the mind rather than the heart and directing its efforts to conditioning its adherants into applying the presuppositions it has adopted as the fundamental substance of itself.

As necessary for a genuine freedom of heart and mind, the Assembly demands an absolute respect for personality as a key principle of its operation. It demands individual loyalty, irrespective of whether this may seem worthily directed or not, and repudiates not only (1) all forms of indoctrination in which man's free choice is denied complete full play and encouragement but also (2) all anarchistic neglect whether wittingly or unwittingly of every person's fundamental obligation to common roots in his culture or his normal relations with his kind. Individuality is taken at its best as always functioning in a most delicate and living balance within the virtually undefinable but yet universal complex of reality. It most importantly rejects the easy answers of popular metaphysical speculation.

To facilitate classification of the Sabian project in the history of philosophy, it might be helpful to borrow the simple system employed by some of the ancient Greeks to distinguish their various systems of thought from each other. They found it convenient to classify on the basis of what each thinker suggested might be that element of which everything would fundamentally be the product. It was an early employment of the principle of evolution, or the idea that all the endless varieties of everyday reality have developed out of one single original and simple something. With Thales this was water. With Anaximander it was an infinite atmosphere and with Anaximenes more specifically air. In a sense and along this line, with Heraclitus it was change or ceaseless activity, and with Pythagoras it was order or pure number. Here of course was no more than mental perspective, and in modern life a commonplace although popularly supposed at times to be a literal description of actualities. Thus the materialist sees everything evolving out of primitive or undifferentiated atoms, or the like, and the religious individual has great comfort in the conception of a divine energy that brings everything into being by magical fiat and thereupon remains capable of a continued control of all eventuality.

Here is the basic or overall metaphysics to which every human mind, in order to preserve its balance or even its sanity, must give some measure of acceptance. It is the womb of total self-existence. In the familiar terms of this sort of ultimate ordering, just what is the primary element out of or within which everything in a Sabian realization can be seen conveniently to have its being and development?

The answer is: CONSCIOUSNESS.

The essence of the common definitions of consciousness is inward awareness, or an intangible something more than the purely private response of mind and body to an accustomed stimulus. In practical fact it virtually defies any definitive description, as for that matter do such terms as BEING or INFINITY or even SELF. These all identify what obviously and actually constitutes them, but without really revealing the nature of what that may be with any absolute preciseness. The value of this philosophical substream of consciousness, emerging in that role in Sabian analysis and exposition through the slow or step-by-step establishment of the project and its materials, is that its employment is equally acceptable to individuals whether leaning toward the materialistic or the transcendental extremes of their own personal metaphysics. Here then is no more than a designation of a given and illimitable relevance, or of a root concordance through which all things and all events have relationship of varying value with all possible phases of each other.

Consciousness so conceived becomes at long last the overall concept in the Philosophy of Concepts. Its elevation now to such a point of special primary in the Sabian exposition might seem to be a puzzling distortion of the very extensive

consideration of the whole group of these conveniently
pivotal terms during an earlier period in the gradual development of the Assembly's fundamental perspective. It
might indeed appear to upset the *1001 Concepts,* and also
to invalidate the previous and much lesser role given to
consciousness, as merely one of a particular eight-key designation, in both the original *Key Truths of Occult Philosophy* published in 1925 and the later refinement of this
schematism in the subsequent *Occult Philosophy* issued in
1948 and presented as largely a complete rewriting and expansion of the preceding analysis. None of this is true in
any respect.

The special emphasis of this now especially emphasized
key truth of occultism, in what is a later stage in the gradual
refinement of Sabian realization and method, is no more
than a broader utilization of the basic insights. The book
Key Truths was the foundational statement of what in due
course came to be identified as Sabian philosophy, and this
initial stage of the general project or vision was brought to
an early climax with the publishing of the *Ritual of Living*
five years later. The occult axiom was first given the form
"consciousness is substance" and this was essentially identi-
cal with the present more narrowly defined "consciousness
is substratum." Actually in presenting the original series,
this one of the key concepts was clearly identified as more
valuable than the others.

It is in such a fashion that the Sabian Assembly has continued to press ahead in its characteristically organic development. In 1929 the mandate from the Great White
Lodge, that in the occult manner of explanation had
charted the group enterprise in its formative California

days, was to begin a new phase for the specific purpose of countering the troublesome overemphasis of the esoteric factors that had helped launch the project preliminarily in late 1922. This led to an objective culmination in 1948, with the far more sophisticated *Occult Philosophy,* in which the special axiom became "consciousness is reality." In the effort to give this latter of two related books on occultism an integrity of its own and the more exoteric ordering, the mandate was not carried out with too great nicety since the intention had been to let *Key Truths* go out of print and to discontinue its publication permanently. Consequently the axioms in *Occult Philosophy* were in part reconstructed.

Meanwhile what has become a very real problem during rather recent years, in the normal growth of the Sabian project, has been the increasing impossibility for many of the students in acolyte discipline to set up the five years of service as a definite monitor in consciousness except on a more and more meaningless basis. The earlier Sabian study groups had a ramification of practical functions over which a personal concern was quite easy to develop, and so to define very precisely. Every active member of the Assembly was charged to do something tangible and regular for the benefit of his fellows no less than himself. His required work in consciousness could be a sustainment of this. With so large a part of the Assembly's membership now consisting of students afield, more and more acolytes have been compelled to choose what for them may remain purely subjective matters for their support in discipline. Gradually this has settled down to a choice quite often of one of the Twelve Plans of Sabian integration, and unhappily it can soon become an ungrounded meditation of very little effectiveness.

What complicates the proposition here is the curious pseudo-literacy coming to characterize modern times. Words are beginning to have a tangibility of idea over and above the fact of what they designate or endow with a name. They are reified. Their repetition would then be felt to be an activation of whatever they represent, forgetting that anything of consciousness must have some manifestation of itself outside of mind to constitute any reality of a sharable or common and valid sort. A much more commonsensical and deeper grasp of the nature of WORK IN CONSCIOUSNESS is becoming a vital necessity at this point in the Assembly's progress. In consequence, as possible approach to the needed perspective, it can be suggested that true meditation is like the phenomenon of the old-fashioned whip top that is kept spinning by the regular flip of the end of a lash in the hand of whoever spins it. This parallels the rhythmic pulse that is the basis of livingness per se. In the Orient for ages such a needed rhythm of power-of-the-self has been cradled or magnified by supportive muscular stability or control to gestate the dynamic of the desired more spiritual end in view, but in modern and especially Western lands the phrenetic accentuation of all life provides the needed factor in much the same way. That is, gestates the strong foundational or psychological self-effort. Repetition of word as image or idea must give way to the faithful reiteration or rhythm of concern.

An illustration of the potency that can be developed in self-rhythm is provided very handily by children whose exceptional need for attention, even of the slightest sort, is almost a first necessity of any healthy ongoing during the immature years of dependence on their elders. The latter have their reward in a perpetuation of their flesh and blood. Growing up, each child will find other reassurances of life to serve the same purpose, but to some extent such a personality support is always needed at core and as a result man anthropomorphises and courts by his worship the sustainment of a sort of whip-top flip of a divine parenthood or something like it. In lesser dimension this psychological symbiotic relationship continues in many variant forms. Thus for no more than the friendly pat or affectionate poke more or less casually through the days of their camaraderie, a man's dog will fight to the death in protecting him. The lady rests, since she is very tired, and when her beloved life-companion passes through the room and brushes back her hair with his hand she smiles without waking and sleeps on all the more wonderfully. The sending of flowers, or the thoughtful telephone message and everything of this general order, are illustration of the whip-top phenomenon in the deeper nuances of consciousness. The technique is increasingly disciplined sentiment.

Work in consciousness is thus infinitely more than the mere shuffling of word or idea in the mind, although all too frequently this is what it has been threatening to become. The maintaining of creative concern in Sabian discipline must avoid the purely mechanical motions to which virtually anything is so easily reduced, as the Buddhist prayer wheel or most dramatically the performance of even sacred rituals by rote. When an acolyte chooses something for meditative support that he cannot comprehend in a genuinely creative envisionment, or as what cannot be a soul-stirring challenge in some phase of his life, his effort will be futile and he may soon feel ever more empty for his pains. There must be somewhere, in his selection of an area of interest, a definite tangibility over which to be concerned to a really vital extent. It must be legitimate, in the sense that he has full respect for personality, and so is not attempting to live the life of somebody else without permission to do so in the particular detail. He cannot employ occult persuasion to compel action by his fellows according to his conception of matters, which of course is black magic. But when he elects participation in a healing ministry, to give aid in consciousness to individuals in misery and difficulty who ask for it, the activity of course is white magic.

What each of the Twelve Plans represents is a phase of Sabian activity into which it is possible to focus an endless occult concern. Most simply this could involve assistance in the conduct of meetings, or any tangible detail of the group enterprise, as in preparing materials or editing them and distributing them in literal actuality since in such a case the help can be objectively grounded as was particularly possible in the earlier years. But it can be a sustainment of intangibilities, as in the whip-top operation of genuine concern without any necessity of actual personal contact or physical participation. Necessary however is the essential sentiment, and that can be built by imaginative rehearsal of the idealized potentials of whatever subjective contribution can actually assimilate into the rhythm of the enduring substance of something. Needed of course is a thoroughgoing acquaintance with the common functions thus given the private and secret but effective strengthening.

Originally the Twelve Plans were no more than a preliminary classification of perspectives, given a convenient statement before the pattern of possible strands of collec-

tive integration had begun to have any formulation in actual practice. This was very much before any possible
thought of shaping them so that an individual assimilation
into their potential development could become an esoteric
involvement in the acolyte and legate procedures. They
now have been restated in a perhaps more rhythmic form,
to facilitate such a ritualistic use of them, and this represents the only actual re-editing in the main text of the
Manual for the 1976 reprinting. The letters of imprimatur, as originally assigned, are maintained as no less cor-
rectly indicative of the threads of invisible sponsorship in
the Sabian vision. The new acolyte has had the benefit of
his approximate initial two years in the discipline to note
which of these threads in the group's fundamental division
of labor may seem to have special application to his case.
If one or several of them have been marking his progress,
or indicating the lessons he may have been studying and
so on, they might give a subtle mark of occult rapport on
which to count if for discipline purposes he chooses a Plan
for his accentuated creative concern.

What has become another very real problem, in the continuing activity of the Sabian Assembly during the past
decade or so, is the matter of the neophyte and other forms
of pledge to which signature is asked in the administration
of the discipline. These were shaped for the earlier and
general situation when the predominant group meetings of
a local sort were possible, and as already noted there seems
to be the possibility of a turn back to that pattern if perhaps in quite modified form and therefore no reason for
radical change in the long-established practices. What might

be a most unhappy move would be to substitute procedures more suitable at this time but proving to be so only very briefly. Rituals traditionally gain their power as they survive in a rewarding use, and to modify them at intervals could encourage a gradual dilution of their effectiveness.

A temporary solution of this problem for a number of years has been to give each new member of the Assembly the mimeographed sheet explaining the present manner of interpreting the pledged obligation. The essence of this special instruction is that the aspirant, when unable to meet any of the literal discipline requirements in the changing world, should on honor work out action and attitude that in his own judgment amounts to a fair and adequate substitute since on page 106 of the main section of this text it is pointed out that all activities in the Assembly must be autonomous, and that they must have "every liberty of modification and non-conformity." There are suggestions throughout the manual's presentation of various ways in which the rituals may be employed. The whole Solar initiation is made up of options that can be taken from the very beginning, such as studying astrology or ignoring it and in due course entering into the acolyte work or refraining from doing so. Other special activities are always open to participation.

Actually there are no usually fixed requirements of performance, in any part of the Sabian discipline, that cannot be altered by the aspirant who feels himself unable to conform to some particular detail. But while he is told that he may prepare a procedure for his own use to further the goals of the group effort, he is warned that such a course

means that he may ultimately become the loner and thereupon have little or no real part in the everyday or common
fellowship. His special way of going in no way means the
least exemption from the living obligations as a whole to
the group of which he makes himself the exceptional part,
since without overall conformity to them the larger entity
will forfeit its special existence. Thus he is expected to
understand that while everything put down in this manual
and elsewhere in Sabian materials is fundamental sugges-
tion, rather than exaction to be accepted without question,
such policy nonetheless is designed to develop the individual's immortal potential and to dramatize the cardinal
initiate personality on which the overall vision must rest.
In other words, as a person he thereby gains additionally
for himself and what is thus gained in the fellowship must
be shared ultimately with his fellows in one fashion or
another.

Moreover, nothing can be permitted in any particular
case that is wholly objectionable to the others among whom
there must be the overall rapport to enable all to function
collectively. There are established standards of the culture,
and the prevailing legal strictures that may actually be en-
forced in any given political or socioeconomic entity. While
reform and change are needed in human life, they properly
come most successfully and enduringly through compatible
association. Differences must be dramatized sufficiently to
arouse at least a general interest since then they made a
broad contribution to all. Indeed, a Sabian member of
marked capacity as a leader might develop a considerable
subgroup of those who have special areas of concern in

which to specialize themselves within the larger teamwork and so increase a worthwhile and wider benefit. This in the new Aquarian Age is the pattern of total cosmic reality, with the expanded interweavings ramifying endlessly on every level.

A third major problem in retaining for now the main text of the 1957 *Manual* is the matter of the recommended reading for the aspirant's background realization. Some of the books at present suggested are difficult if not impossible to get on loan or by purchase. The *Hidden Way Across the Threshold* for all its beauty is hopelessly outdated, and is no longer really worth attention. Any attempt to solve the difficulty by revision of the listings when the *Manual* is reprinted would be defeated in these modern times because of the continual changes in the occult and allied literature even in a single year or so. These recommendations in consequence will be omitted in the book's future revisions, and in the meanwhile a frequently updated small brochure will be printed for use throughout the group as soon as it is possible to prepare it. It will be known as *Collateral Reading for Sabian Students* and will be reasonably comprehensive with brief accounts on each entry and selective listings of (1) general material in which there is common Sabian reference, (2) material good for supplementing Sabian studies and (3) material of parallel or widely general interest but not recommended for reasons that will be given.

To be noted is that now the *Sabian Book* rather than the mimeographed *Sabian Fundamentals* is given to each newcomer as he makes his affiliation with the Assembly. The latter however is available by purchase.

REISSUE OF PHILOSOPHY LESSONS

Sabian year of presentation	Date of first lesson in series	Title of series (When 27 lessons, so indicated)
Second Cycle		
41st	1963, Oct. 14	Plotinus: Reality
	1964, Apr. 13	Art of Being
42nd	Oct. 12	Aristotle: Taxonomy
	1965, Apr. 12	Art of Wisdom
Third Cycle		
43rd	1965, Oct. 11	Plato: Republic
	1966, Apr. 11	Grimm's Fairy Tales (27)
44th	Oct. 17	Ibn Gabirol: Source of Life
	1967, Apr. 17	Blavatsky's Secret Doctrine
45th	Oct. 16	Plotinus: Ethics
	1968, Apr. 15	Olympian Concepts
46th	Oct. 14	Plato: Socrates
	1969, Apr. 14	Life Technique (27)
47th	Oct. 20	Aristotle: Psychology
	1970, Apr. 20	Life Analysis
48th	Oct. 19	Plotinus: Cosmology
	1971, Apr. 19	Tools of Intelligence
49th	Oct. 18	Aristotle: Physics
	1972, Apr. 17	Tools of Insight
50th	Oct. 16	Plato: Atlantis
	1973, Apr. 16	Tools of Inspiration
51st	Oct. 15	Aristotle: Logic
	1974, Apr. 15	1001 Nights

52nd	Oct. 14	Plotinus: Destiny
	1975, Apr. 14	Omar's Quatrains
53rd	Oct. 13	Aristotle: Metaphysics (27)
	1976, Apr. 19	Studies in Alice
54th	Oct. 18	Plato: Banquet
	1977, Apr. 18	Fictional Symbolism
55th	Oct. 17	Aristotle: Ethics
	1978, Apr. 17	Elementary Signatures
56th	Oct. 16	Plotinus: Personality
	1979, Apr. 16	Sabian Psychology
57th	Oct. 15	Aristotle: Politics
	1980, Apr. 14	First Principles
58th	Oct. 13	Plato: Athens
	1981, Apr. 13	Renaissance of Thought
59th	Oct. 12	Aristotle: Aesthetics
	1982, Apr. 12	Modern Thought (27)
60th	Oct. 18	Plotinus: Idealism
	1983, Apr. 18	Art of Play
61st	Oct. 17	Aristotle: Biology
	1984, Apr. 16	Art of Duty
62nd	Oct. 15	Plotinus: Reality
	1985, Apr. 15	Art of Being
63rd	Oct. 14	Plato: Republic
	1986, Apr. 14	Art of Wisdom
64th	Oct. 13	Aristotle: Taxonomy
	1987, Apr. 13	Grimm's Fairy Tales (27)

Fourth Cycle

65th	1987, Oct. 19	Ibn Gabirol: Source of Life
	1988, Apr. 18	Blavatsky's Secret Doctrine
66th	Oct. 17	Plotinus: Ethics

	1989, Apr. 17	Olympian Concepts
67th	Oct. 16	Plato: Socrates
	1990, Apr. 16	Life Techniques (27)
68th	Oct. 22	Aristotle: Psychology
	1991, Apr. 22	Life Analysis
69th	Oct. 21	Plotinus: Cosmology
	1992, Apr. 20	Tools of Intelligence
70th	Oct. 19	Aristotle: Physics
	1993, Apr. 19	Tools of Insight
71st	Oct. 18	Plato: Atlantis
	1994, Apr. 18	Tools of Inspiration
72nd	Oct. 17	Aristotle: Logic
	1995, Apr. 17	1001 Nights
73rd	Oct. 16	Plotinus: Destiny
	1996, Apr. 15	Omar's Quatrains
74th	Oct. 14	Aristotle: Metaphysics (27)
	1997, Apr. 21	Studies in Alice
75th	Oct. 20	Plato: Banquet
	1998, Apr. 20	Fictional Symbolism
76th	Oct. 19	Aristotle: Ethics
	1999, Apr. 19	Elementary Signatures
77th	Oct. 18	Plotinus: Personality
	2000, Apr. 17	Sabian Psychology
78th	Oct. 16	Aristotle: Politics
	2001, Apr. 16	First Principles
79th	Oct. 15	Plato: Athens
	2002, Apr. 15	Renaissance of Thought
80th	Oct. 14	Aristotle: Aesthetics
	2003, Apr. 14	Modern Thought (27)
81st	Oct. 20	Plotinus: Idealism
	2004, Apr. 19	Art of Play

82nd		Oct. 18	Aristotle: Biology
	2005, Apr. 18	Art of Duty
83rd	Oct. 17	Plotinus: Reality
	2006, Apr. 17	Art of Being
84th	Oct. 16	Plato: Republic
	2007, Apr. 16	Art of Wisdom
85th	Oct. 15	Aristotle: Taxonomy
	2008, Apr. 14	Grimm's Fairy Tales (27)

Fifth Cycle

86th	2008, Oct. 20	Ibn Gabirol: Source of Life

REISSUE OF BIBLE LESSONS

Date of first lesson in series	*Title of series* (Noted when other than 24 lessons)

Third Cycle

1965, Feb. 8	Promised Land (48)
1966, Jan. 10	Mosaic Covenant (48)
Dec. 12	Mosaic Prophecy (48)
1967, Nov. 13	Studies in Matthew (34)
1968, July 8	Wisdom Gospel (45)
1969, May 19	Passion Week (56)
1970, June 15	Magical Message
Nov. 30	Epic Message
1971, May 17	Thaumaturgic Message
Nov. 1	Legalistic Message
1972, Apr. 17	Ritualistic Message
Oct. 2	Civil Message
1973, Mar. 19	Pauline Theology

Sept. 3	Pauline Eschatology
1974, Feb. 18	Pauline Mysticism
Aug. 5	Pauline Authority
1975, Jan. 20	Pauline Idealism
July 7	Pauline Humanism
Dec. 22	Hebrew Destiny
1976, June 7	Hebrew Worship
Nov. 22	Hebrew Suffering
1977, May 9	Hebrew Politics
Oct. 24	Hebrew Vision
1978, Apr. 10	Hebrew Oracles
Sep. 25	Prophetic Source
1979, Mar. 12	Prophetic Power
Aug. 27	Prophetic Judgment
1980, Feb. 11	Prophetic Wisdom
July 28	Prophetic Deliverance
1981, Jan. 12	Prophetic Knowledge
June 29	Evangelical Origins
Dec. 14	Evangelical Growth
1982, May 31	Evangelical Vision
Nov. 15	Evangelical Consummation
1983, May 2	Evangelical Fortitude
Oct. 17	Evangelical Achievement

Fourth Cycle

1984, Apr. 2	Promised Land (48)
1985, Mar. 4	Mosaic Covenant (48)
1986, Feb. 3	Mosaic Prophecy (48)
1987, Jan. 5	Studies in Matthew (34)
Aug. 31	Wisdom Gospel (45)
1988, July 11	Passion Week (56)
1989, Aug. 7	Magical Message

1990, Jan. 22	Epic Message
July 9	Thaumaturgic Message
Dec. 24	Legalistic Message
1991, June 10	Ritualistic Message
Nov. 25	Civil Message
1992, May 11	Pauline Theology
Oct. 26	Pauline Eschatology
1993, Apr. 12	Pauline Mysticism
Sep. 27	Pauline Authority
1994, Mar. 14	Pauline Idealism
Aug. 29	Pauline Humanism
1995, Feb. 13	Hebrew Destiny
July 31	Hebrew Worship
1996, Jan. 15	Hebrew Suffering
July 1	Hebrew Politics
Dec. 16	Hebrew Vision
1997, June 2	Hebrew Oracles
Nov. 17	Prophetic Source
1998, May 4	Prophetic Power
Oct. 19	Prophetic Judgment
1999, Apr. 5	Prophetic Vision
Sep. 20	Prophetic Deliverance
2000, Mar. 7	Prophetic Knowledge
Aug. 22	Evangelical Origins
2001, Feb. 5	Evangelical Growth
July 23	Evangelical Vision
2002, Jan. 7	Evangelical Consummation
June 24	Evangelical Fortitude
Dec. 9	Evangelical Achievement

Fifth Cycle

2003, May 26	Promised Land (48)

GENERAL INDEX

Sadducees, 129
Salvation, 74, 82, 129
Sanskrit, 17
Science, 68, 107, 174
Science and Health, 55
Screen of prophecy, 84, 100
Secrecy, 40
Secret Doctrine, 52
Self, doctrine of (SEE ALSO laya center) , 12, 77, 171
Semiannual meetings, 152
Senses, 123
Sentiment, disciplined, 290
Sermon on the Mount, 119
Servant Songs, 71, 145
Seton, Julia, 28
Sexual continence, 35
Sheba, 19
Shrine, healing, 113
Signature books, 139
Signatures, 18, 176
Silence, (SEE ALSO entering) , 117, 143, 190
Sin (moon god) , 20
Sinai, 121
Socrates, 167
Solar Breath, SEE Meditation on
Solar Mysteries, 9, 13, 15, 23, 31, 39, 52, 57, 61, 65, 71, 74, 76, 80, 83, 87, 103, 105, 112, 128, 144, 153, 156, 158, 171, 174, 177, 197, 232, 238
Solar myth, 141
Solar path, 11, 16, 39, 118, 127, 144, 155
Solomon, 19
Soul, 69, 87
Source of Life (Fons Vitae), 77
Spark, divine, 60
Spiritualism and psychic procedures, 21, 23, 33, 39, 49, 55, 56, 85, 89, 111, 124, 150

Sports, 112
Statements of Realization and Thanks, 137, 143, 229, 234, 240
Steiner, Rudolph, 53
Stephens, Robert, 146
Stimulants, 35
St. John the Baptist, 19
Street, J. C., 55
Student, SEE aspirant
Students afield, 42, 283, 288
Study group, 42, 108, 161
Study procedure, 32, 76, 97, 103, 108
Substance, 18, 62
Sumerian, 19, 22, 147
Survival (SEE Spiritualism) , 59, 201
Tarot, 18, 49, 102
Temple, invisible, 215, 246
Temple of the People, 23
Thales, 285
Thanatos, 61
Theosophical Society (Adyar) , 23
Theosophy, 18, 21, 23, 49, 53, 83, 147
Thought Form, 17
Tobacco, 35, 111
Torah, 97
Tower of Babel, 75
Trine, Ralph Waldo, 55
Truth (SEE New Thought) , 72, 171, 174
Unction, 125
Vedanta, 51
Vicarious function, 73, 82, 95
Visitors, 108, 138, 157
Volunteer workers, 27
Vowels, sacred, SEE intonation
Welcoming Address, 153, 245
Wesak festival, 118
Wheeler, Elsie, 23
Whip-top phenomenon, 289
White letters, 101
Wisdom, SEE eternal